NOVELLI

A Forgotten Sculptor

JOSEPHINE MURPHY

BRANDEN BOOKS
Boston

Library of Congress Cataloging-in-Publication Data

Novelli, a forgotten sculptor / Josephine Murphy.
   p. cm.
Murphy, Josephine.

Includes bibliographical references and index.
   ISBN 0-8283-2076-4 (alk. paper : ppk.)
    1. Novelli, James, 1885-1940.
    2. Sculptors — United States —Biography.
    3. Public sculpture — New York (State) — New York.
    I. Title.
NB237.N68 M87 2002
730'.92 — dc21

2002005031

BRANDEN BOOKS
Division of Branden Publishing Company
P.O.Box 812094
Wellesley MA 02482

To the memory of MAMIE MELFA,
her legacy of love kept the memory
of her brother alive.

"Are not all things born to be forgotten?"
—George Borrow
Lavengro Chapter XXV

1. *James S. J. Novelli*, 1903. (Photo: courtesy of the Melfa family).

ACKNOWLEDGMENTS

I am indebted to Michael Melfa, for agreeing to be interviewed for this book and providing me with information about his family. My thanks also go out to other members of the family: especially Felix Melfa, Renée Melfa, Felix Novelli, and Frances Melfa for the time they spent answering my incessant questions and our many pleasant telephone conversations. Above all this book has been enriched by the immeasurable memories handed down by Mamie Melfa, to her children, before her passing.

This book would not have been possible without the support of a score of dedicated researchers from a myriad of libraries and institutions across the United States, who spent countless combined hours locating answers to my reference questions. Contributions were made by Anne Berkley, Head of Reference and Carol Passmore, Business Reference Librarian, Durham County Library; Judith Walsh, Division Chief Brooklyn Collection/Brooklyn Public Library; Anne Louise Bayly and Elizabeth Botten, Reference Services Librarians, Archives of American Art Smithsonian Institution; Jane Rupp, Director, Marion County Historical Society; Kevin Kuharic, President, Gate City Caretakers; Tom Pellegrene Jr., Manager of News Technologies at *The Journal Gazette*, Ft. Wayne, Indiana; and Sachiko Onishi, Photo Archivist, City of New York Parks & Recreation Department.

I wish to mention gratefully and thank formally the following:

For their gracious assistance in granting me access to their archival materials — Gwen Pier, Executive Director, National Sculpture Society; Katherine Romero, Deputy Director, Art Commission of the City of New York; Jonathan Kuhn, Director of Art & Antiques and Karen Lemmey, Monuments Coordinator of Art & Antiques, City of New York Parks & Recreation Department.

For their willingness to give research assistance in obtaining photographs and reproductions — Karin Strohbeck, Archivist/Librarian, Amon Carter Museum; Joan Stahl, Image and Electronic Resources Administrator, Smithsonian American Art Museum; Teresa Harris, Program Associate, The Architectural League of New York; Judy McCollough, Historical Archive Manager, Marshall County Museum; Ida H. Chipman; Alicia Martin; Greg Murphy, President, Awesome Sounds Productions; Shirley Katzter, Coleridge School; and Evelyn Weeks, Assistant Executive Director, Great Falls Regional Chamber of Commerce.

For providing assistance and know-how in the area of computer technology — Ron Murphy, President, RM760 Consulting.

For expert proofreading performed with utmost integrity — Daniel Gelinas.

For suggesting I write about an Italian-American sculptor — Professor Angelo Tripicchio, Robert J. Kibbee Library, Kingsborough Community College.

I am grateful to my family and friends for their patience and understanding, especially my granddaughters Brittney and Sydnee.

Special thanks to my husband, Bill, for his loving support and immeasurable help with locating the sculptures of James Novelli.

CONTENTS

ILLUSTRATIONS

1. *James S. J. Novelli*, 1903. (Photo: Melfa Family).
2. *Victory,* Saratoga Park War Memorial, 1921, Brooklyn, New York. (Courtesy: The Architectural League of New York).
3. *My Grandmother*, Sulmona, Italy, 1904. (Photo: Peter A. Juley & Son Collection, Smithsonian American Art Museum).
4. Novelli & Calcagni, *Chief Menominee Monument*, 1909, Marshall County, Indiana. (Photo: Ida H. Chipman).
5. *America Triumphant*, Pershing Field War Memorial, 1922, Jersey City, New Jersey.
6. *Sir Walter Raleigh*, c 1929. (Courtesy: National Sculpture Society).
7. *Untitled* [Allegorical Figure]. (Photo: Peter A. Juley & Son Collection, Smithsonian American Art Museum).
8. *Victorious America,* Winfield World War Memorial, 1926, Queens, New York. (Photo: Greg Murphy, Awesome Sounds Productions).
9. *Clason Point War Memorial*, 1928, Bronx, New York. (Photo: Peter A. Juley & Son Collection, Smithsonian American Art Museum).
10. *Aviator* [Spirit of Flight Sculpture] 1928. (Photo: Peter A. Juley & Son Collection, Smithsonian American Art Museum).
11. *Spirit of Flight*, 1928, Fort Wayne, Indiana. (Photo: Peter A. Juley & Son Collection, Smithsonian American Art Museum).

27. *Abraham Lincoln* [Standing] 1929. (Photo: Peter A. Juley & Son Collection, Smithsonian American Art Museum).
28. *Untitled* [Equestrian]. (Photo: Peter A. Juley & Son Collection, Smithsonian American Art Museum).
29. *Untitled* [Shipwrecked]. (Photo: Peter A. Juley & Son Collection, Smithsonian American Art Museum).
30. *Untitled* [American Indian]. (Photo: Peter A. Juley & Son Collection, Smithsonian American Art Museum).
31. *Gloria Bartnett Memorial.* (Photo: Peter A. Juley & Son Collection, Smithsonian American Art Museum).
32. *Untitled* [Female Nude with Cymbals]. (Photo: Peter A. Juley & Son Collection, Smithsonian American Art Museum).
33. *Untitled* [Female Nude]. (Photo: Peter A. Juley & Son Collection, Smithsonian American Art Museum).
34. *Untitled* [Female Nude]. (Photo: Peter A. Juley & Son Collection, Smithsonian American Art Museum).
35. *Torso*, 1931. (Photo: Peter A. Juley & Son Collection, Smithsonian American Art Museum).
36. *Memorial Door, Mrs. C. LaGioia*, 1923, Calvary Cemetery, New York. (Courtesy: The Architectural League of New York).
37. *Memorial Door, Hon. Peter Schmuck*, 1921, Woodlawn Cemetery, New York.
38. *Memorial to Thomas James Stewart*, 1923, Woodlawn Cemetery, New York. (Courtesy: The Architectural League of New York).
39. *Rowan Panel*, c 1920, Woodlawn Cemetery, New York.
40. *Memorial Door, Edward Siegman*, 1920, Woodlawn Cemetery, New York.
41. *Memorial Door, John Lordi, Esq.,* 1924, Calvary Cemetery, New York.
42. *Memorial Door, DeSalvio,* 1937, Calvary Cemetery, New York.
43. *Memorial Door, Antonio Latorraca*, 1938, Calvary Cemetery, New York.
44. *Memorial Door, Bernard F. Golden*, 1930, Calvary Cemetery, New York.

2. ***Victory***, Saratoga Park War Memorial, 1921, Brooklyn, New York. Sculpture: Bronze 8'x2'6"x1' (Base/Stele: Milford pink granite). (Courtesy, The Architectural League of New York).

1

REDUCED TO RUBBLE

April 21, 2000

F OR almost eighty years *Victory* (fig. 2), a sculpture by
James Novelli (1885-1940) stood diligently on its pedestal
in Saratoga Square Park in the Bedford-Stuyvesant section of
Brooklyn. First approved by the New York City Art Commission May 5, 1920, the monument was designed as a war memorial to commemorate the young soldiers of the neighborhood who had sacrificed their lives defending the country
during World War I. The Saratoga Park statue depicted an allegorical female figure of "Peace and Victory" installed against a
stone stele. She wore a laurel wreath and held up a palm
branch in her right hand. Her left arm came to rest along the
top of a shield inscribed with the phrases "E PLURIBUS
UNUM / IN MEMORY OF THE HEROIC DEAD BY RESI-
DENTS DISTRICTS 31-32 OF THE CITY OF NEW YORK
A.D. MCMXXI."[1] The monument was no stranger to vandal-
ism; the large bronze tablets that once accompanied the statue
and bore the names of the Brooklyn military personnel killed,
had been stolen in 1974. The final degradation came in the
early morning hours of April 21, 2000, when two thieves, using
a blowtorch, ruthlessly removed the 1,000-pound statue from
its base. The career criminals were soon apprehended, but not
before the sculpture had been chopped up into 300 pieces, in
preparation for being melted down.[2] The original price for the
statue was $5,500; it is estimated it would cost between

$80,000 and $100,000 to recreate in today's market. *Victory* was cast by the Roman Bronze Works of Greenpoint, Brooklyn, a reputable foundry of the time which in addition to executing many of Novelli's sculptures, produced some of the sculptures and monuments at Rockefeller Center, including the famous Prometheus fountain.[3]

2

AN ARTIST REDISCOVERED

READING about the theft in *The New York Times* was my first encounter with the sculptor James Novelli. The news article had captured my attention and my curiosity was aroused: who was this man and what could history divulge about the artist who had designed this now lost sculpture? Browsing through reference books and art history books was of surprisingly little help; there was practically nothing written about this artist except for a brief biography which occupied about a quarter of a page and included a very short inventory of his work.[4] With this small amount of information in hand, I began my quest by looking through annual newspaper indexes, hoping to locate articles that would document the ceremonies surrounding the unveiling of his monuments and indirectly shed some light on the sculptor. The research was long and te-dious but definitely worth the effort; by my following up on each minuscule lead, slowly the life and personality of the art-ist, along with his works, began to evolve. Good fortune and several unexplained coincidences also played major roles in my research. A most important breakthrough occurred when two nephews of the sculptor, Michael and Felix Melfa, got in touch with me and graciously consented to an interview. Over-all, the information that I was uncovering both disturbed and intrigued me. I was transported into a unique period of history, a time between the great World Wars, a score of years filled with extremes: prosperity and depression, peace and anxiety, jubilation and sorrow. In a similar manner these disparities would be echoed in the life and work of the artist James Novelli. This book will present, for the first time, a comprehensive overview of the diverse sculptures of this talented, Italian-American artist. It will attempt to reconstruct the critical circumstances surrounding his life and assess their effects on the character of the sculptor and the nature of his works. However, to fully understand the social climate of the era and the artistic influences that prevailed during the early period of Novelli's maturity as an artist, we must first go back over a hundred years and start at the end of the nineteenth century.

The *Gilded Age*, that dynamic period between the end of the Civil War and the beginning of World War I, was an extremely productive era for the advancement of American sculpture. The success of the Philadelphia Centennial Exposition of 1876 inspired similar commemorative events in other cities. These many extravagant expositions were paramount in contributing to the public's awareness of sculpture as an art form, and the demand for sculptural commissions was occurring at an unprecedented rate. Public sculptures ennobling the citizenry and celebrating military and civic accomplishments practically dominated the early part of the twentieth century. The allure of this thriving and lucrative art market convinced an extraordinarily large number of artists to channel their talents toward sculpture — until the number of sculptors swelled to an unparalleled proportion. Many a young artist of this time, eager as they all were to make a name for themselves, was caught up in this profusion of opportunity. So many, in fact, that over the years history has lost sight of their names and the countless works they created. This is the story of one such artist who was influenced by the *Gilded Age* and prospered during the *Roaring Twenties*, only to experience firsthand how an enthusiastic public attitude could turn unpredictably to one of indifference.

3

SETTLING IN AMERICA

I am an American. This is the country of opportunity. If any man says he can't get a chance here, I just ask him to read the life of Abraham Lincoln and take a new grip on himself ...Nothing is impossible here.

— James Novelli, 1922

JAMES SALVATORE JOHN NOVELLI (fig.1), was born on October 15, 1885 in Sulmona, a town in the province of Aquila, in central Italy.[5] When he was five, his family immigrated to America and, like many Italian-Americans, settled in New York City. Upon their arrival, in February of 1890, his parents Felice (Felix) and Lucia rented rooms in a five-story tenement at 34 Mulberry Street, in the area now known as "Little Italy." The family would spend the next several decades living on Mulberry Street, moving only one house down from where they originally settled. James remained an only child until the age of ten when his sisters, Anna and Josephine, were born in 1895 and 1897, respectively. Not long afterwards the siblings were joined by two brothers, Frank in 1899 and Charles in 1901, and yet another sister, Mamie in 1906. Throughout her life, this youngest child Mamie would always look up to her oldest brother James, holding him in the highest esteem. The personal memories that Mamie handed down to her sons, Michael and Felix, along with faded newspaper clippings about her beloved brother, have provided us with the most intimate information about the artist James Novelli.

While a young student attending Public School 23, then located at 70 Mulberry Street, James would take chalk from the classroom blackboard and create sidewalk drawings. Impressed by this display of natural ability, both his parents and his teachers encouraged his artistic talents.[6] By a stroke of luck, a wealthy gentleman happened to see his work and took an interest in this amicable young man. As a result, in 1903, when he was eighteen years old, means were afforded him for study in Europe, and he enrolled at the Royal Academy of Fine Arts in Rome.[7] Even though many expenses of the Academy were paid for by his benefactor, Novelli's parents also had to contribute towards his training. They were by no means well off: his father Felice worked as a street cleaner for the New York Department of Sanitation, and his mother Lucia worked as a seamstress in what is known as a sweatshop. They were determined to make sure that their eldest son, of whom they were very proud, had the means to complete his studies at the Academy. Even the older children were expected to find small jobs and contribute their salaries to help pay expenses for the advancement of their oldest brother's career.[8]

At the Academy Novelli studied under many notable European artists and masters of public sculpture, such as Guilio Monteverde, Ettore Ferrari, and Silvio Sbricoli.[9] He learned to paint as well as sculpt in the strict academic style. He studied anatomy and learned the techniques of modeling in clay and plaster and the carving of stone, particularly marble.

On his occasional days off from school, he would often travel east from Rome to his birthplace of Sulmona to visit his grandparents. It was sometime during 1904, on one of those visits, that he modeled the portrait bust *My Grandmother* (fig. 3). Undoubtedly, he possessed the skills necessary to become a fine sculptor, for even at this early stage of his training, this work conveys an extremely fine quality of expressiveness and to a certain extent an essence of animation. While still a student, in 1906, he competed and won honorable mention at the International Exposition held in Paris. He graduated from the Royal Academy of Rome in 1908.

Three years earlier on October 6, 1905, Felice Novelli, accompanied by his friend and sponsor, Giuseppe Albano, had walked eagerly into the District Court of the United States for the Eastern District of New York. This was a very special day for Felice, one he had been anticipating for a long time; proudly he took the Oath of Allegiance, making him and his family citizens of the United States, and thereby fulfilling his dream.

James, too, was filled with that pride to be an American. An ardent admirer of Abraham Lincoln, he would often refer to Lincoln's biography and look to him as a role model. For Novelli, there were no restraints to becoming successful, only those that were self-imposed. He sincerely believed that anything was possible in this country; opportunities were plentiful, and he was confident that he would soon be a success.

3. ***My Grandmother***, Sulmona, Italy, 1904. Whereabouts unknown. Portrait bust: Terra cotta. (Photo courtesy of the Peter A. Juley & Son Collection, Smithsonian American Art Museum #J0115496).

4. Novelli & Calcagni, ***Chief Menominee Monument***, 1909, Marshall County, Indiana. Sculpture: Granite 7'x3'6"x3'6" (Base: Granite). (Photograph by Ida H. Chipman).

4

THE EARLY YEARS

BACK in the United States, following his graduation, he began working as a marble cutter to put together the necessary funds to purchase materials for his sculptures. He soon moved up the ladder of success to his next position, that of an assistant to a sculptor who had a studio on Broadway. Obviously, his artistic talent had not gone unnoticed, for just a few years later commissions began to come his way.

On one of his earliest jobs, working under the direction of the designer Frank Southworth, Novelli and another artist by the name of Calcagni, jointly fabricated the *Chief Menominee Monument* (fig. 4), located near Plymouth, in northern Indiana.[10] The granite monument is a full-length heroic portrait of Chief Menominee (1791-1841), arrayed in full Potawatomi regalia, gazing across the land that once belonged to his people. The statue, commissioned with a $2,500 legislative grant, was dedicated on September 4,1909, to commemorate the removal of those Indians from their reservation on September 4, 1838. The monument was the first memorial that any state had ever erected to an Indian. Even today, almost a hundred years later, the statue of Chief Menominee remains a tourist attraction and a symbol of historic importance, so much so that the people of Marshall County have placed a photo of the sculpture on the first page of their telephone book. Historian James M. Mayo, wrote about the sculpture, suggesting that this remembrance demonstrates "local pride in Indian history" while giving "an air of legitimacy to the removal of the Indians."[11]

It must have become apparent to Novelli that he would be able to make a good living in his chosen field of art. The nation's victorious role in World War I kindled an overwhelming feeling of nationalism, and even before the end of that Great War there was a renewed nationwide demand for memorials and monuments. Americans felt an awe-inspiring need for visible symbols to express what they needed to remember: death, sacrifice, sorrow, victory and gratitude. Having studied in Rome with Guilio Monteverde, a master sculptor who obtained numerous commissions for funerary memorials and monuments celebrating national heroes,[12] Novelli was well trained and prepared to give the public what it wanted. Novelli, had established a reputation as a well-known sculptor, enough so that in the early part of the1920s he decided to open his own studio at 400 West Twenty-third Street in Manhattan. He entered numerous competitions, of which he won several, including an award for his War monument *Victory*, the sculpture that would bring him recognition as a brilliant young sculptor.

5. ***America Triumphant***, 1922, Pershing Field, Jersey City, New Jersey. Sculpture: Bronze painted gold 8'x4'x2', on a rock base.

5

STATUE MAKERS

T HE war was over, the country was heading into the *Roar-ing Twenties* and money was plentiful. The overall impact of the war on the economy had been beneficial. As is always the case in a prosperous economy, people had the money to indulge in the luxury of the fine arts.

It was also a time when a sculptor, unless looked upon as exceedingly famous, was more likely to be thought of as a craftsman, a statue maker. Historically, the populace, in its evaluation of the arts, had always placed sculpture in second place after painting. Professional sculptors, like Novelli, referred to their work as "sculpture" whereas architects, politicians and the general public mostly used the term "statue." Yet, it was during this time that memorials were typically dedicated with great pomp and ceremony. Events surrounding the unveiling of these memorials were always thoroughly planned and orchestrated.

Such was the case when, in 1922, Novelli's memorial *America Triumphant* (fig. 5), was unveiled at Pershing Field, Jersey City, commemorating the 147 neighborhood soldiers who had died in the War. The statue depicts an allegorical female figure dressed in classical garb that stands holding an inscribed full-length shield at her front left side and in her crossed arms carries a bundle of palm branches.[13] The dedication ceremony took place on Independence Day, and a crowd watched in awe as an airplane circled overhead for two hours and at timed intervals dropped a rose to the ground until 147 roses, each one representing one man who had died, formed an immense bouquet at the foot of the monument.[14] *The New York Times* covered the pageantry and reported the details of the event along with the names of the invited dignitaries. However, there is neither mention nor credit given to the "statue maker," James Novelli. His work was treated merely as a purchase; something one buys and shows off with no thought given to the originator.

A similar scenario had ensued with the unveiling of his Saratoga Park memorial *Victory,* on September 11, 1921. A short article in *The New York Times* stated that more than 2,000 persons were present at the ceremony: a detachment of the Thirteenth Coast Defense Command, the 106th Infantry Post, 244 Veterans of Foreign Wars and principal speakers Senator Charles Lockwood, Borough President Edward Riegelmann, Judge George Martin and District Attorney Harry Lewis, but once again no mention was made of the sculptor.[15] One cannot help but wonder if Novelli was even present at the ceremony, or how he felt about a major newspaper ignoring his part in the creation of the monument.

6

A RISING STAR

J AMES NOVELLI was elected to the membership of the National Sculpture Society (NSS), in 1922, at a time when the honorary president of the Society was the eminent sculptor, Daniel Chester French. Since its inception in 1893, and for decades to follow, members of the National Sculpture Society were considered the most important sculptors at work in the United States. The Society's aim was to "spread the knowledge of good sculpture"..."encourage the production of ideal sculpture for the household and museums," and indeed to "... promote the decoration of public buildings, squares and parks with sculpture of high class."[16] The creation of the National Sculpture Society stemmed from the sculptors' desire to achieve greater strength for their profession. Although sculptors looked to the NSS for professional advancement, they realized that to an extent their influence was limited and that there was a vital need to build upon associations with other professional and civic groups in order to get the necessary backing, prestige and clout they desired. Therefore from the outset, non-sculptors such as architects, painters, lawyers and businessmen, were invited to become members of the National Sculpture Society thus forming the basis of their major support.

The NSS called for the establishment of standards for competitions and strict criteria for artistic performance that would distinguish the highly trained professional sculptor from the commercial modeler and stone-carver. Admission to the society required a nomination by a member and an acceptance vote from the whole group; in this manner they were able to exclude undesirable candidates.[17] The Society provided sculptors with opportunities for work and for establishing their reputations. NSS members consistently secured the best and richest commissions available, and their works dominated public spaces throughout the 1920s. The *Exhibition of American Sculpture Guide: April 14th-August 1st* (revised edition of 1923) documents that James Novelli, exhibited three of his works along with the noted sculptor Frederic W. MacMonnies.[18] Also from April to October 1929, Novelli exhibited in *Contemporary American Sculpture: the California Palace of the Legion of Honor* at Lincoln Park in San Francisco (fig. 6).[19]

By 1922, Novelli was evidently an accomplished artist with a promising future in this flourishing sculptural market. His *Victory* memorial and *America Triumphant* had introduced him to an appreciative public and brought him recognition as a talented young artist. Taking stock of these early accomplishments, he was quoted as saying, "When I look back at last year and see the great strides I have made, I know I am on the way to success." A year later in 1923, at the age of 38, he married Marie Magdalena (Lillian) Simeone, a remarkably attractive young woman with raven black hair, and on August 29,1924 their only child, James Felix Joseph Novelli was born; his parents called him "Jimmy".

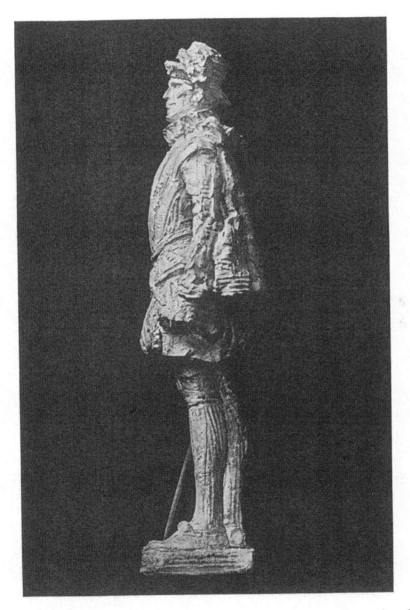

6. **Sir Walter Raleigh**, c 1929, Whereabouts unknown. Reproduced from *Contemporary American Sculpture: the California Palace of the Legion of Honor*, 244. (Reprinted by permission of the National Sculpture Society).

7. **Untitled** [Allegorical Figure], Whereabouts unknown. (Photo courtesy of the Peter A. Juley Collection, Smithsonian American Art Museum #J0115497).

7

SCULPTOR OF MONUMENTS

THE creation of a public sculpture normally involved many stages: the establishment of a fund-raising and supervisory committee, the solicitation of donations from organizational members, or even the initiation of a city- or nation-wide subscription campaign. Once the necessary funds were collected, a sculptor was chosen either by a panel of experts or maybe by a competition. The selected sculptor would then sign a contract either with the monument committee or the head of the municipal department under whose jurisdiction the sculpture was to be placed; in New York City this was usually the Department of Parks. The sculptor would then work up a set of designs and a small-scale model to be approved by the monument committee or in the case of work planned for city property, by the Art Commission of the City of New York. Upon approval, the sculptor would then enlarge his model to full scale before it was sent to the foundry to be cast in bronze.[20]

Monuments were usually modeled on academic conventions of representation inspired by classical art, and sculptors considered allegory an essential part of their vocabulary. The sculpture on the previous page (fig.7), is typical of the kind of allegory being utilized during the period in which Novelli worked. Note for example the palm leaf the figure is holding aloft in her right hand, a symbol of victory, and in her left she is gripping a shield and sword, the accoutrements identified with a warrior. The allegorical female figure is modeled on the exploits of Minerva (Athene), the goddess of wisdom and war, but, unlike her male counterpart Mars, Minerva always fought on the side of justice. On her head rests a crown made of laurel leaves, distinctively reserved for those individuals worthy of honor. Since the time of ancient Rome paintings of victorious generals have been depicted wearing a crown of laurel leaves.[21]

As we have already seen in reviewing works that Novelli created for the Great World War, classical allegory played an important role in public monuments. Probably no monument played a more prominent role than that most famous public sculpture, the *Statue of Liberty*. At the time no one questioned whether allegorical representation in sculpture could translate into practical ideas and values. Artists and the educated community that backed public art, assumed that the American general public would understand the lessons conveyed through these allegorical works. When in fact, not everyone was able to relate to these civic sculptures and eventually, this idea of allegory would become a problematic issue.

Victorious America, better known as the Winfield World War Memorial (fig. 8), another of Novelli's works dedicated to the valiant soldiers of the First World War, was erected on May 30, 1926, at Laurel Hill Boulevard and 65th Street, Woodside, Queens. Approved by the Art Commission of the City of New York,[22] it was paid for through voluntary contributions by the citizens of the Winfield Honor Roll Association of the Borough of Queens and donated to the Department of Parks. Novelli's design once again utilizes a larger than life-sized allegorical female figure representing "America." The artist's description of the sculpture states that she stands holding with her left hand a shield, symbol of protection, good government and honor, whereupon is inscribed a dedication paying due tribute to the men who made the supreme sacrifice for their country. Her right hand rests on the symbolic sword that fought for freedom's cause, and she wears a long flowing dress, a detailed breastplate and a laurel wreath on her head. "Joy and vigor are registered in this figure because the principles of democracy were saved; for peace and reconstruction are to follow."[23]

The Winfield World War Memorial, that today stands in Woodside, Queens, was Novelli's second attempt at a design for this monument; his first submission in March 1922, had been disapproved by the Art Commission.[24] It is interesting to note that five years later the same design, which had been rejected by the Art Commission for the Winfield Memorial, was then approved, by the Art Commission for the *Clason Point War Memorial.*

The *Clason Point War Memorial* (fig. 9), located at Woodrow Wilson Square, Clason Point, Bronx, was commissioned by the Clason Point War Memorial Committee and donated to the city. It was a collaboration with the architectural firm of A.H. Bowie & Son, of Long Island City. Dedicated in 1928, the large bronze relief tablet represents an allegorical female figure of "Victory," unfolding the American flag that symbol of freedom that has been defended since the founding of the country. In the statue's right hand are found the "...tablets of law and order, basic ideals that our fathers have fought for, and that in the late war [were] upheld heroically."[25] Topped by an American Bald Eagle with outspread wings, the monument is inscribed, "DEDICATED TO THOSE WHO MADE THE SUPREME SACRIFICE AND TO ALL OTHERS FROM CLASON POINT WHO ENTERED THE SERVICE OF OUR COUNTRY IN THE WORLD WAR."

The *Victory Memorial Fountain,* also known as the Corona Heights War Memorial, Queens, was originally erected in a small neighborhood park, situated on a triangular patch of land, bounded by Corona Avenue, 108th Street and 51st Avenue. Officially approved by the Art Commission on September 13, 1927, it cost $5,500 and was donated to the City Parks Department from the citizens of the Corona Heights Civic Association. According to the blueprints and a description of the monument written by James Novelli, the fountain consisted of a large circular granite water basin in the center of which stood a ten-foot high cylindrical granite monument supporting bronze panels which were separated by Doric columns. The panels depicted, "...the American nation paying homage and tribute to the patriotic spirit and sacrifice of the American soldier of the World War."[26] Regrettably, the years had not been kind to the monument; decay, vandalism and pollution from heavy traffic eventually took its toll on the memorial fountain. Longtime residents of the neighborhood recall memories of the fountain, remembering how as children they would play in the basin, which for many years no longer held water, and the fun they had climbing atop the center of the monument. As is the way of progress, over three decades ago the old park along with the fountain was torn down and a new park was erected in its place; a bocce ball court now replaces the *Victory Memorial Fountain*, as the focal point of the park.

Novelli's reputation as a sculptor extended beyond the New York area; lucrative commissions came in from cities throughout the United States. The *Spirit of Flight* (fig. 10), a memorial to Arthur R. Smith, known as "Bird Boy" of the U.S. Mail Service, was erected at Memorial Field, Fort Wayne, Indiana. This pioneer aviator was killed in a crash on February 12, 1926, after encountering a heavy snowstorm while transporting the mail between Bryan and Monteplier, Ohio. Dedicated on August 15, 1928, the monument features a bronze figure of a male nude standing on tiptoe atop a sphere with arms outstretched at shoulder height and wings attached to his arms. This pose was not uncommon and had been used by other sculptors. What makes this statue unique are the many identifying accessories the artist provides for his figure. The airman wears a 1920s aviator helmet and his face is turned upward to the sky; also shapes, possibly clouds, encircle him modestly. Often in ancient Rome, great events or individuals were celebrated by the erection of columns. Where at first the simple column had been considered a powerful enough motif, now these elaborate memorials were created. Utilizing the language of classicism, Novelli's sculpture is mounted atop an estimated twenty-five-foot-high granite column set upon a squared base (fig. 11). The base features four bronze relief panels, one on each side. The front panel depicts an anvil, two ladies, an airplane, an animal, smokestacks and a tire; the left panel, illustrates an airplane, a steamboat, an Indian and an angel; the rear panel shows two men driving a stagecoach containing two passengers; and the right relief panel depicts an Indian watching a steam locomotive.[27] The memorial stands as an inspiration to the coming generation and a symbol of Art Smith's courage and his skyward dream.

The *Rockingham War Memorial,* (fig. 12), in Bellows Falls, Vermont, was dedicated in 1927, to commemorate those "WHO MADE THE SUPREME SACRIFICE AND TO ALL OTHERS FROM THE TOWN OF ROCKINGHAM WHO ENTERED THE SERVICE OF OUR COUNTRY IN ALL THE WARS." Novelli's allegorical "Lady Liberty" stands proud against a granite column. The apex of the column, shown flat and undecorated in an earlier picture, was later embellished with an American Bald Eagle with outspread wings (fig 13). The granite female figure in this monument is similar to the bronze allegorical figure representing "America" in the *Winfield World War Memorial* dedicated a year earlier in Woodside, Queens (see fig. 8).

The *Soldier's Monument* (fig. 14), in Veterans Memorial Park in Lockport, New York, erected in 1930, was a collaboration with Lockport artist, A. Raphael Beck. Here once again we see the designer's use of the classical vocabulary to express the magnitude of the military sacrifice being memorialized. The awe-inspiring obelisk-like pillar of the *Soldier's Monument* is topped not by the traditional pyramidal form but instead by James Novelli's impressive seated bronze sculpture "Lady Liberty." The allegorical figure wears a World War I combat helmet and holds a staff with the Lockport nameplate crowned with a small eagle. Ornate bronze torches that once decorated the four corners of the base were later vandalized and removed. The original bronze plaque at the base of the monument is inscribed with the phrase "ERECTED IN MEMORY OF THOSE WHO MADE THE SUPREME SACRIFICE AND TO ALL OTHERS WHO SERVED IN THE WARS OF THE UNITED STATES."[28]

8. ***Victorious America***, Winfield World War Memorial, 1926 Laurel Hill, Queens, New York. Sculpture: Bronze 7' (Base: Stoney Creek granite). (Photograph by Greg Murphy, President, Awesome Sounds Productions).

9. ***Clason Point War Memorial***, 1928, Clason Point, Bronx, New York. Relief tablet: Bronze 6'x3' (Photo: courtesy of the Peter A. Juley & Son Collection, Smithsonian American Art Museum #J0115522).

10. **Aviator** [Spirit of Flight Sculpture] 1928, Novelli's studio, 400 West
Twenty-third Street, New York. (Photo courtesy of the Peter A. Juley
& Son Collection, Smithsonian American Art Museum #J0115519).

11. **Spirit of Flight**, 1928, Fort Wayne, Indiana. Sculpture: Bronze 8'x6'x2'6" (Base/Column: Barre granite 25'). (Photo courtesy of the Peter A. Juley & Son Collection, Smithsonian American Art Museum #J0115493).

12. ***Rockingham War Memorial***, 1927, Bellows Falls, Vermont. Sculpture: Granite, against a granite column. (Photo courtesy of the Peter A. Juley & Son Collection, Smithsonian American Art Museum #J0115489).

13. **Rockingham War Memorial** [with eagle on top] 2001. (Photo courtesy of Evelyn Weeks, Great Falls Regional Chamber of Commerce).

14. **Soldier's Monument**, 1930, Lockport, New York. Sculpture: Bronze, atop the column. (Photo courtesy of the Peter A. Juley & Son Collection, Smithsonian American Art Museum #J0115491).

8

A VERSATILE SCULPTOR

O F all his works, it is in his traditional portrait bust that it is
   most evident that Novelli made a sincere and genuine attempt to capture, in clay, an insight to the true personality of
the sitter. He aimed for a real understanding of the nature and
character of the subject before executing the sculpture. Even
after the work was begun, if he was not completely satisfied
with the work in progress, he would destroy the piece entirely.[29] The viewer needs only to look into the face of *My
Grandmother* (see fig. 3), particularly the eyes, to readily see
the sitter as a real presence. It is as if one can sense the entire
physical person just by looking at her head and neck. His
grandmother's face exhibits both the struggle, which comes
from years of hard work and the strength that stems from de-
termination. Both these features seem to defy the fragile frame
of the elderly woman. The sculptor is accentuating the com-
plexity of the human character that is inherent in all individuals. We can see the same understanding of human nature in the
sculpture, *Study of an Old Man* (fig. 15), whose weather-beaten
face provides the viewer with an insight into what must have
been the harsh life of the sitter, while his placid features communicate a mellow disposition. Similar complexities are present in the bust of *My Father* (fig. 16). The many years of
working outdoors had taken its toll on his face, carving furrows
in his forehead and turning his skin to a leathery texture.
Though the subject presents a gentle demeanor, the sculptor
has also captured his unique spirit. In a manner of detached

captured his unique spirit. In a manner of detached presence, the sitter gazes directly into the eyes of the spectator, thus turning the tables on the viewer. The subject's eyes impart very little information about himself; rather he appears to be scrutinizing the viewer. The latter two portrait sculptures were exhibited at the Annual Exhibition of the Pennsylvania Academy of the Fine Arts: the *Study of an Old Man* in 1916 and *My Father* in 1932.

Novelli's most poignant and emotional bust is that of an unknown young woman (fig. 17). Reminiscent of the casualness and spontaneity of a Baroque work, the sculpture incorporates the neck and shoulders of the sitter, leaning them ever so slightly forward. A most vocal piece, the lips are slightly parted as though to speak and her expressive eyes appear as if to be imploring an unseen presence. Truly an animated sculpture, having the ability to touch the very soul of the viewer. Conversely, his portrait bust of *Abraham Lincoln* (fig. 18), is much less revealing, embracing a more professional mannerism. The president is shown very much in control, presenting an attitude of strength and leadership. The face by itself, disengaged from its neck or shoulders, is shown to be a very powerful tool for human expression. This is especially true when looking into the face of Christ (fig. 19). Neither vocal nor animated, in its own quiet manner this sculpture forces the viewer to experience an air of humility when confronted with this image. Although posed in a frontal position, the portrait bust does not make eye contact with the viewer. The half opened, half closed eye-lids place the viewer at a psychological disadvantage. Without the benefit of looking into the eyes, the very window of the soul, the spectator is left with little alternative but to stare into the face of the statue seeking to penetrate the psyche of the subject.

By the second decade of the twentieth century a new class of wealthy people had emerged: newly famous financiers, celebrities, actors, and musicians who came to regard themselves as figures important enough to warrant portraits. Novelli's work by this time had become well known, and orders for portrait busts came in from many sides, not just for the famous alone but also for their wives and children. Some of Novelli's successful busts are of *Julius Berger, Irving Green, Margaret Lawson, Anita Novarra, Peter Anderson*[30] *and Leo Tolstoy.* The artist also won a competition for his bust of *Warren G. Harding* (fig. 20), for the Harding Memorial in the hometown of the late President at Marion, Ohio.[31] In addition, he produced a number of portrait reliefs, most notably of *James Cardinal Gibbons, Charlotte Brainard, Charles G. Brainard, Dorothy Langley, Dora Ford, Francis P. DeLuna,*[32] and *William B. Drake.*[33]

A half-length bronze relief plaque honoring *John R. Rathom* (fig. 21), hangs above a fieldstone fireplace in the Rathom Lodge at Camp Yawgoog, Rockville, Rhode Island. It was dedicated on the 4th of July 1929, John Rathom's birthday. Editor of *The Providence Journal*, Mr. Rathom was considered the father of the Boy Scouts movement in Rhode Island.[34] Using varying degrees of relief, the portrait of John Rathom, shown in profile, is dressed in the official attire of the Boy Scouts and set against an inscribed background surface. The inscription on the left side of the portrait records Rathom's last message to the Boy Scouts and to the right is a dedication to the man himself. Around the border of the sculpture and also embossed within the inscription we find assorted accoutrements associated with the Boy Scouts. The billowy camp fire with its long curl of smoke, imprinted within the message to the right of the portrait, is the symbol used by the Rhode Island Boy Scouts. Wrapping three sides of the perimeter are 48 stars, representing the forty-eight states which made up the United States at that time; this was to give emphasis to the fact that the Boy Scouts were a nationwide organization. The four shields on the bottom of the border are replicas of the Rhode Island Boy Scouts' emblem. Embossed within the inscription are "palms" in the form of a feather and an arrow, together symbolizing the highest achievement attainable in the Boy Scouts.

Richard P. Rooney (fig. 22), Grand Trustee of the B.P.O. Elks and President of the New Jersey State Elk's Association died in December of 1929 at the age of 57. A delegation of members from the Elk's Newark Lodge #21, desiring to dedicate a memorial to Mr. Rooney, contacted the General Bronze Corporation and negotiated the price for a life-sized bust to be created for the occasion at the cost of $1,000. The General Bronze Corporation informed the group that they would have the model executed by a well-known sculptor and to the satisfaction of the committee.[35] James Novelli contracted for the assignment and was to receive a $500 commission, $250 of which was to be credited toward Novelli's account because the sculptor still owed the General Bronze Corporation $500 for castings they had recently executed for him. The foundry later reconsidered their offer and decided they would credit the entire amount of $500 toward Novelli's account. Initially Novelli agreed to this arrangement; however, the year was 1930, only a few months after the Stock Market crash of 1929 and the sculptor had taken a severe loss in the market. Novelli decided to take a different tack when on January 21, 1930 the Elk Lodge Committee called at his studio on West Twenty-third Street to inspect the model for the bust of Mr. Rooney. He presented his deal directly to the committee explaining that he could deliver the model cast in bronze for about $200. Also, he told the committee he could supply them with a full-length statue for $1,000, the same amount General Bronze was asking for just the bust.[36] The Committee from the Elk Lodge contemplated his offer for several days, but in the end decided that they would honor their original deal with General Bronze. The bust of Richard P. Rooney was duly completed and shipped to the Newark Elk Lodge on May 29, 1930.[37] This incident can be interpreted, as members of his family have suggested, that the stock market crash was starting to have an effect on the sculptor's finances.

Even during the initial years of the Great Depression there were a large number of wealthy patrons who could still afford sculpture and who desired to embellish the gardens on their private estates in a fashion similar to that of public parks and gardens. In April of 1931, a bronze bust of *Lord Byron* (fig. 23) was commissioned for the estate of Francis M. Jesta, a prominent attorney of Manhattan Beach, Brooklyn, New York. The owner being of Italian heritage and an ardent admirer of Romantic poetry placed the bust in the front garden of his 1927 Italianate style house, where it remained for over a half a century. The bronze life-sized bust of Lord Byron became a landmark in the neighborhood and a symbol for the private elementary school that later occupied the site. According to Mrs. Shirley Katzter, principal, when the school purchased the property, it actually integrated the statue into its formal name, changing its name from the Coleridge School to the Coleridge School Byron Campus. Unfortunately the bust was stolen from its base on April 2, 1984.[38]

James Novelli was a versatile artist, his success with monuments endorsed his position as an artist, and when opportunity offered, he proved himself equally a master of the portrait sculpture. Although the tradition of portrait sculpture in America was shaped in the middle of the eighteenth century through the influences of European sculptors, American sculptors at the turn of the twentieth century brought a new quality of energy and naturalism to portrait sculpture. To better recreate the subtle nuances inherent in naturalism, bronze soon became the medium of choice; bronze was also much more durable and better suited for outdoor sculpture.

These naturalistic qualities can be readily observed in many of Novelli's portrait sculptures, such as *Columbus* (fig. 24), erected in 1928, in West Side Park, Jersey City, New Jersey. This figurative sculpture of Columbus stands in a fairly relaxed contrapposto, on a traditional tiered pedestal, commonly used at that time. Communicating an aura of sophistication, his right hand rests on his hip and his right leg extends forward and is slightly bent at the knee. His stance non-verbally interprets his demeanor as one of confidence and leadership. The facial features exhibit a haughty look of satisfaction, while his eyes look afield in a compelling sweep, surveying the far distances, beyond the viewer's immediate vicinity. He uses this same stance and relaxed manner for his clay model of a Colonial Officer, perhaps the likeness of George Washington (fig. 25).

The World War I memorial titled *Flanders Fields*, 1927 (fig. 26), was to be erected on Hudson Boulevard, Jersey City, New Jersey. Relying heavily on body language, the sculptor was able to impart to the viewer the figure's most intimate thoughts through his exterior form. With hat in hand, the lone doughboy's pensive expression and downcast head, generates a poignant reminder to the general public of all the young men who had served their country and fallen in their prime. Truly an emotional tribute that was meant to give pause and induce thought within the mind of the viewer.

Mr. Novelli's *Abraham Lincoln*, (fig. 27), stands perfectly still. Shaded details of his face reveal the character of the man and his frame of mind at the moment being represented. The slightly drooped head and the quiet mood communicate a genuine expression of feeling. There are no dramatics; his hands are not raised in gesture; on the contrary, his burly fists at his sides express the intensity of his meditation. The artist has managed to penetrate the facade of the presidential guise and gaze into the very soul of the man, exemplifying his dignity, seriousness and to a certain extent his vulnerability.[39]

At the opposite extreme is Novelli's much more dramatic and animated equestrian sculpture of a dashing and courageous Calvary Officer (fig. 28), the likeness of which appears to be that of Teddy Roosevelt. The figure no longer stands alone upon its pedestal; the dynamic rider sits astride the advancing horse, awakening the imagination of the viewer, summoning visions of an army being led to the forefront of a battlefield. The horse, though vaguely startled, appears solid on its feet and the figure sits confidently upon the animal. There is a sense of spirit and life in both the horse and the rider, accentuated even further by the commanding vitality in the lifted arm. The hoof of the horse's hind leg is exactly under the center of his body, producing a perfect balance the axis of which extends upward through the body of the rider uninterrupted to the tip of his sword. The total equestrian mass is thereby perceived as a symmetrical entity and is shown in a good relationship to the simple narrow base.

Often art and literature have worked hand in hand, one feeding off the other for inspiration and aesthetics. In Homer's *Iliad* can be found the early concepts of landscape art in its detailed description of the amazing shield of Achilles. Then again during the latter part of the thirteenth century, literature was first on the scene to experience the renewed appreciation of nature. The return to nature extolled in the writings of St. Francis, Dante and Petrarch found its parallel in the paintings of the artists of the Italian Renaissance. So does it seem that literature may have influenced Novelli to create his untitled work, which I call *Shipwrecked* (fig. 29). Daniel Defoe's novel *Robinson Crusoe*, had always enjoyed widespread recognition among the reading public. Although waning somewhat in the 1850s, by the 1900s there was a renewed acclaim for the book, which was considered a masterpiece. The classic story of a shipwrecked mariner describes the struggle suffered by one man to which many could relate. Novelli's sculpture could very well be his visual interpretation of the premise of the story. Several comparisons between the novel and the sculpture can easily be made. For example, alongside the figure are the remnants of a ship's broken mast and rope, Robinson Crusoe is portrayed in the book as having been marooned on an island after his ship encountered a violent storm, and stranded with little more than the broken remains of the ship. Looking at the ship's mast, one can see the metal rings that hold the wood together, this type of mast was used on sailing ships during the 17th and 18th centuries. The seaman depicted is wearing a loose fitting shirt and rolled up pants, possibly pantaloons, clothing that would have been worn in the time period in which the story takes place. The author describes the sole survivor as a tall and strong young man with long hair; Novelli in a similar manner, defines the muscular tone of his figure and emphasizes the details of the body through the opening of the torn shirt. Seagulls alighting and tall waves crashing against solid rocks provide the sculpture with its sublime setting.

Novelli was at one time interested in the subject of the American Indian (fig. 30); perhaps this sculpture stemmed from his work on the *Chief Menominee Monument,* either as a study for that monument or afterward. In either case, he renders the figure of the Indian in a more archaic style, reversing his usual trend for naturalism. Though the face and head of the figure are depicted in a naturalistic manner, they appear to contain the typical features which were ascribed to Indians during that time: straight hair, high cheek bones, deep set eyes and tight lip jaw. It's surprising to note that no attempt was even made to produce a sense of naturalism with the body of the figure; it seems to be influenced solely by the desire to produce a vision of brute strength through its archaic frontal stance. It is possible that Novelli was swayed by society's popular concept of what Indians were like, whereby most people perceived them as angry savages and different from themselves.

The nude figure, especially the female figure, has always been a subject of interest to artists, extending back to antiquity. The majority of nudes have generally been created with the purpose of representing the ideal figure. A most famous American example was Augustus Saint-Gaudens' *Diana,* which stood from 1892 until 1925 on the rooftop of the old Madison Square Garden designed by McKim, Mead and White. *Diana,* an allegorical figure, is holding a bow and arrow and is positioned balancing one foot on a sphere and the other raised outwardly behind her. Placing this nude figure of a woman in a public place caused quite a sensation in the tabloids of its time. Novelli certainly must have been aware of this sculpture and may have even been influenced by it to a certain extent. In his memorial to *Gloria Bartnett* (fig. 31), can be found a pose similar to that of the *Diana*, where the right leg is lifted backward off the ground, leaving the figure to remain balanced on the toes of her left foot. In keeping with the modesty of the day, Novelli is careful to avoid too much detail of the human figure. The female sculpture is deliberately rendered in allegorical form, and the lyre she is holding reinforces the artist's intention that the figure is essentially a statue of a mythological figure and not a nude. The simple inscription on the base reads: I WILL FIND ACRES OF SKY FOR MY DREAMING.

Nudes executed by James Novelli in a more naturalistic manner include: the lady with cymbals (fig. 32), and an angelic-faced woman with her arms folded behind her back (fig. 33), both of which are straightforward interpretations of the standing nude. Whereas, the figure of a woman stretching her arms above her head (fig. 34), can easily be interpreted in more seductive terms. The figure's closed eyes and dreamy appearance lends the sculpture a provocative implication.

Even fragments of torsos have their place in the history of art. From antiquity to modern times, the torso has always been a popular subject for sculptors, not only for their anatomical training but also for their exploration of sculptural appeal, as we can see in the twisting and turning contrapposto of Novelli's nude male *Torso* (fig. 35).

15. ***Study of an Old Man***, 1916, Whereabouts unknown. Portrait bust. (Photo courtesy of the Peter A. Juley & Son Collection, Smithsonian American Art Museum #J0115492).

16. ***My Father,*** c 1923, Whereabouts unknown. Portrait bust. (Photo courtesy of the Peter A. Juley & Son Collection, Smithsonian American Art Museum #J0115488).

17. **Untitled** [Young Woman] Whereabouts unknown. Portrait bust: Clay. (Photo courtesy of the Peter A. Juley & Son Collection, Smithsonian American Art Museum #J0115505).

18. **Abraham Lincoln** [Portrait bust], Whereabouts unknown. (Photo courtesy of the Peter A. Juley & Son Collection, Smithsonian American Art Museum #J0115486).

19. **Untitled** [Head of Christ] Whereabouts unknown. Portrait bust: Clay. (Photo courtesy of the Peter A. Juley & Son Collection, Smithsonian American Art Museum #J0115498).

20. ***President Harding***, Warren G. Harding Memorial, 1924, Marion, Ohio (Unlocated). Life-sized, Portrait bust: Plaster cast. (Photo courtesy of the Peter A. Juley & Son Collection, Smithsonian American Art Museum #J0115518).

21. *Memorial to John R. Rathom*, 1929, Camp Yawgoog, Rockville, Rhode Island. Relief plaque: Bronze. (Photo courtesy of the Peter A. Juley & Son Collection, Smithsonian American Art Museum #J0115525).

22. ***Richard P. Rooney***, 1930, B.O.P. Elk's Lodge #21, Newark, New Jersey. Life-sized, Portrait bust: Bronze. (Photo courtesy of the Peter A. Juley & Son Collection, Smithsonian American Art Museum #J0115494).

23. **Lord Byron**, 1931, Coleridge School Byron Campus, Brooklyn, New York, (Stolen 1984). Life-sized, Portrait bust: Bronze. (Photo courtesy of George and Shirley Katzter, Coleridge School.

24. **Columbus,** 1928, Originally erected in West Side Park [Renamed Lincoln Park in 1930] Jersey City, New Jersey, (Unlocated). Portrait Sculpture: Bronze. (Photo courtesy of the Peter A. Juley & Son Collection, Smithsonian American Art Museum #J0115508).

25. **Untitled** [Colonial Officer] Whereabouts unknown. Portrait Sculpture: Clay. (Photo courtesy of the Peter A. Juley & Son Collection, Smithsonian American Art Museum #J0115503).

26. Detail, *Flanders Fields* [Doughboy] 1927, Originally to be erected on Hudson Boulevard, Jersey City, New Jersey, (Unlocated). Portrait Sculpture: Plaster cast. (Photo courtesy of the Peter A. Juley & Son Collection, Smithsonian American Art Museum #J0115501).

27. **Abraham Lincoln** [Standing] 1929, Whereabouts unknown. Portrait Sculpture. (Photo courtesy of the Peter A. Juley & Son Collection, Smithsonian American Art Museum #J0115500).

28. **Untitled** [Equestrian] Whereabouts unknown. Sculpture: Bronze.
(Photo courtesy of the Peter A. Juley & Son Collection, Smithsonian
American Art Museum #J0115499).

29. **Untitled** [Shipwrecked] Whereabouts unknown. (Photo courtesy of the Peter A. Juley & Son Collection, Smithsonian American Art Museum #J0115526).

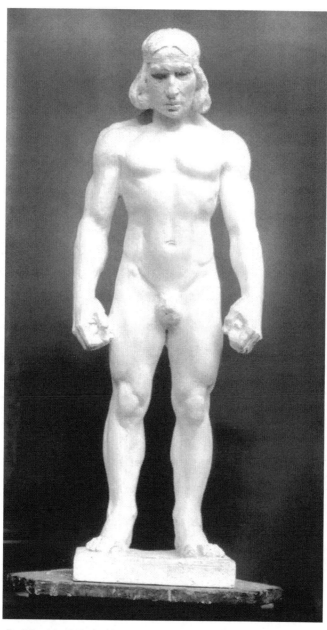

30. Detail, ***Untitled*** [American Indian] Whereabouts unknown. Portrait Sculpture. (Photo courtesy of the Peter A. Juley & Son Collection, Smithsonian American Art Museum #J0115487).

31. ***Gloria Bartnett Memorial***, Whereabouts unknown. (Photo courtesy of the Peter A. Juley & Son Collection, Smithsonian American Art Museum #J0115504).

32. Detail, ***Untitled*** [Female Nude with Cymbals] Whereabouts unknown. (Photo courtesy of the Peter A. Juley & Son Collection, Smithsonian American Art Museum #J0115510).

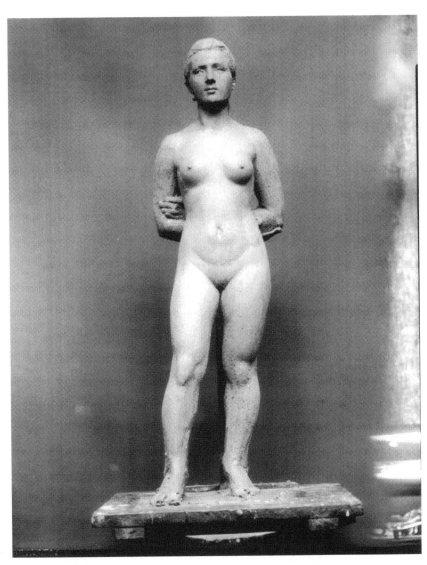

33. ***Untitled*** [Female Nude] Whereabouts unknown. (Photo courtesy of the Peter A. Juley & Son Collection, Smithsonian American Art Museum #J0115506).

34. **Untitled** [Female Nude] Whereabouts unknown. (Photo courtesy of the Peter A. Juley & Son Collection, Smithsonian American Art Museum #J0115509).

35. **Torso**, 1931, Whereabouts unknown. (Photo courtesy of the Peter A.
Juley & Son Collection, Smithsonian American Art Museum #J0115485).

36. ***Memorial Door, Mrs. C. LaGioia,*** 1923, Calvary Cemetery, New York. Mausoleum door: Bronze 40"x79". (Courtesy, The Architectural League of New York).

9

MEMORIALS AND MAUSOLEUMS:

A Dying Art

NOVELLI was also a member of The Architectural League of New York (founded in 1881). Even at the height of his popularity, after the First World War, the sculptor's livelihood often depended on the favor of architects for commissions. The goal of The Architectural League was to promote the ideal of mutual enrichment through collaboration. Muralists, sculptors and many other artists were invited to become members and their annual exhibition included sections for landscape, architecture, painting, sculpture and the decorative arts.[40] From 1922 through 1928, with the exception of 1926, Novelli displayed his sculptural works at the League's annual exhibitions. The outstanding feature of these exhibitions was the strict examination, by jury, that each piece submitted had to pass. To ensure a high standard of merit and secure the best possible results, The Architectural League placed great stress upon originality of design. No reproductions would even be considered.[41] At the Thirty-eighth Annual Exhibition, in 1923, Novell's bronze door intended for the *LaGioia* mausoleum (fig. 36), in Calvary Cemetery, New York won the coveted Henry O. Avery Prize for sculpture.[42] The exquisite design reveals an imposing image of balance and design. The collaborating artist on that mausoleum was the renowned architect Gilbert Stanley Underwood.

A mausoleum door is a form of relief sculpture. Unlike sculpture in the round, which is an independent object, that may be designed to stand in open space, where it can be viewed from all directions, a relief sculpture is totally dependent on its background and is meant to be seen merely from a frontal position. There is a vast range of different kinds of works that are covered by the term '*relief*;' they vary in size from full height figures such as can be found in the great pediment sculptures of antiquity to the portraits found on the smallest of coins. Novelli created a number of different types of relief sculptures; case in point is his earlier work the *Clason Point War Memorial* (see fig. 9), a grand scale relief tablet rendering a larger than life-sized allegorical figure. A most versatile form of art, relief style was put to popular use in portraiture as can be seen in the artist's *Memorial to John R. Rathom* (see fig. 21), and his many other successful relief portraits. Although widely used to commemorate great events and individuals, relief sculpture, as an ancient form of art, was frequently utilized in funerary structures to decorate tombs, gravesites and sarcophagi. Borrowing this idea from antiquity, Novelli translated the ornate classical funerary theme into a somewhat more simplistic language, which conformed itself more readily to meet the needs of a modern society.

The newly risen merchant magnates and financiers of the *Gilded Age* had demanded splendor not only in their homes but also in their final resting place, the mausoleum — a trend that continued well into the 1920s. A good share of the Society "400" chose to be buried at Woodlawn Cemetery, New York and leading architects competed in building grandiose mausoleums for them.[43] Being a member of the Architectural League of New York, Novelli benefited through collaboration with these architects and received commissions to decorate the bronze panels and doors of many mausoleums. Several of Novelli's designs can be found in Woodlawn Cemetery, many of which were displayed at The Architectural League's Annual

Exhibitions. The bronze memorial door designed in 1921 for the *Hon. Peter Schmuck* (fig. 37), depicts a polished gold angel with halo against a painted brown background. The angelic figure implied guidance of the soul of the deceased to salvation. This sculpture was shown in the League's 1922 Annual Exhibition along with his Saratoga Park *Victory* monument. His 1923 memorial for *Thomas James Stewart* (fig. 38), is a bronze statue of a female figure dressed in classical garb, her head bent in a pose of sorrow. The full sized bronze statue stands on a base of pink granite. This memorial sculpture was entered into The Architectural League's 1925 Annual Exhibition. The memorial known as the *Rowan Panel* (fig. 39), is a rectangular bronze relief of two angels kneeling before a cross. The panel is set above two plain bronze doors. The simple inscription on the panel reads, "Blessed are the Pure in Heart for they shall see God." Around 1920 a bronze mausoleum door was designed for *Edward Siegman* (fig. 40). The door portrays a typical classical funerary relief of a female figure with her head bent in mourning, holding a symbolic laurel wreath. The theme for this door is somewhat similar to the memorial door he later designed for *John Lordi* (fig. 41), Calvary Cemetery, which he presented at the 1925 Annual Exhibition. Much more powerful, even more so when seen on location, the *Lordi* mausoleum door is a later and mature version of a classical female figure. The figure, though larger, is more refined and is clearly much more poignantly effective than his earlier image.

Calvary Cemetery, particularly the area known as the St Calixtus Division, Calvary Cemetery No. 1, is the oldest of this four-part cemetery. It contains several mausoleum doors designed by James Novelli, in addition to the two memorial doors, *Lordi* and *LaGioia*, previously discussed.[44] His most beautiful and intricate mausoleum door, reminiscent of a Renaissance work, was designed in 1937 for the *DeSalvio Family* (fig. 42). Recreating the Passion of Christ, he has divided the mausoleum door into the Fourteen Stations of the Cross. Reading the panels from the top left corner down, we can follow the traditional sequence of scenes from the Passion of Christ: Christ is condemned to die; he is charged with carrying the cross; Christ falls for the first time; Christ meets his mother Mary; Simon helps Christ carry the cross; he meets Veronica; Christ falls for the second time. Moving over to the top right and reading downward, Christ meets the women of Jerusalem; he falls for the third and last time; he is being stripped of his clothes; nailed to the cross; crucified; taken down from the cross and finally, placed in the tomb. A cross fabricated with palm leaves divides the two columns while the arms of the Cross are decorated with lilies, a symbol of the Resurrection.

In a similar vein, though on a smaller scale, is the memorial door created for *Antonio Latorraca* (fig. 43), in 1938, situated adjacent to the *DeSalvio* mausoleum. Exquisite in its own right, this mausoleum door also illustrates the Fourteen Stations of the Cross, only this time the panels are designed in the form of a cross, to be read first going downward, the vertical pole of the cross, and then transversely along the horizontal arms. The *DeSalvio* and *Latorraca* doors are by far the most ambitious designs that James Novelli undertook for mausoleums, but they were not by any means the only ones. He created many original, award-winning mausoleum doors. It is no wonder that he was an acclaimed sculptor in his lifetime; his mausoleum doors rank among the most successful within the New York area.

Commissioning a mausoleum was by no means a simple endeavor. Take, for example, the mausoleum built for the wealthy real estate broker, Bernard F. Golden of 51 Maiden Lane, New York City (fig. 44). The commission was initiated sometime prior to 1929 when Mr. Golden first contracted the architectural firm of A.H. Bowie & Sons of Long Island City to draw up the plans for a mausoleum to be located in Calvary Cemetery. A project such as this required a typical collaboration between an architectural firm, a stone contractor to cut the granite for the building, in this case, the Memorials Art Company, a sculptor and finally a foundry. With the approval of the client Mr. Golden, the sculptor James Novelli, was chosen to design the door for the mausoleum. The Roman Bronze Works (RBW) foundry was then selected to cast the sculptor's clay model into bronze, and was also expected to supply the hardware and complete the hanging of the door on its hinges. James Novelli first became involved with this project in the early part of 1929. He immediately set about designing a clay model for the mausoleum door, which had to be approved by his client Bernard Golden. Enclosed within a letter to the Roman Bronze Works, Novelli sent a sketch of the door, with measurements, requesting that they supply him with an estimate for the cost of the casting. On March 12, 1929, the Roman Bronze Works replied with a proposal, in writing, to furnish: one cast bronze mausoleum door approximately 40"x80" with open grill work and hinged glass frame behind grill work; cast bronze saddle and built up bronze door jamb; all necessary hardware, to be set in place, for the sum of $900.00.[45]

Acting upon the approved order, the Roman Bronze Works wrote the architectural firm of A.H. Bowie requesting that they supply them with their plans and dimensions for the mausoleum; the casting of the doors depended upon the plans of the architect. It was also at this time that the Memorials Art Company wrote the Roman Bronze Works, requesting the exact measurements of the door frame so that they could cut the granite accordingly.[46] However, on May 28th the Roman Bronze Works wrote to Mr. Golden, stating that the architect's drawings submitted for the mausoleum failed to contain the dimensions that were requested, thereby delaying the progress. Trying a different approach, on June 12[th,] the Roman Bronze Works telegraphed the Memorials Art Company for the dimensions on the architectural drawings they maintained. There seemed to be a discrepancy in the dimensions, so in the end the Roman Bronze Works sent a letter to James Novelli, stating that they would establish the dimensions themselves and submit the drawing to the owner and to the stone contractor, who would then have to follow them accurately. Any expense involved in making changes, should the door not fit the opening in the stone work, would be borne by the owner.[47]

An unforeseen obstacle posed a further problem. It was necessary for the Roman Bronze Works to inform Mr. Golden of the strike that occurred in their industry on May 15th affecting the plants of the bronze and iron foundries in their territory. It is interesting to read that the foundry reassured Mr. Golden that their men, in general, had no grievances and made no demands. However, a "Communistic Association not recognized by any of the labor organizations forced a number of our men to stay out and the rest have remained away through fear."[48] The Communist Labor Party in the United States was small but vocal. Many Americans, at that time, interpreted the nation's problems as being the product of Communist infiltration rather than the natural consequences of an economy readjusting itself. Unfortunately, there is no correspondence dating the exact end of the strike. But it obviously did not last too long because on June 27th the Roman Bronze Works submitted their completed drawings of the bronze door for final approval by Mr. Golden; work should have begun immediately, but, once again, work on the project was delayed, due this time to the fact that the Roman Bronze Works had never received an approval from Mr. Golden. By July 18th after four more letters and repeated telephone calls, the RBW had still not heard from Mr. Golden. In their final letter, dated August 7th the RBW informed Bernard Golden that work on their contract to furnish a bronze mausoleum door had been suspended owing to the fact that they had not heard from him. Furthermore, due to Mr. Golden's failure to cooperate, the RBW could no longer guarantee to maintain the agreed upon schedule of completion (April 24, 1930).[49] Although there is no record of correspondence, sometime prior to October 1929, Mr. Golden must have approved the drawings and work was under way once more but with yet another twist in the schedule. This time, work was held up due to a change in the granite by orders from the Memorials Art Company. On December 5th with the change in granite out of the way, final approval was given to complete the door. However, before they could do so, the Roman Bronze Works on January 20, 1930 once again wrote to Bernard F. Golden, stating that his order for one mausoleum door at the sum of nine hundred dollars ($900.00) was approximately one half completed at this time. In accordance with their usual custom on all orders of this size, they now requested that half the balance, $450.00, be sent to them. It wasn't until March 10th after continually following up, that the RBW finally received this payment, making them, of course, concerned about receiving their final payment in a timely fashion. It was for this reason that RBW decided to request final payment prior to shipment of the mausoleum door.[50]

In keeping with their original scheduled time of completion the bronze mausoleum door was ready by April 21st at which time final payment was received and on April 24, 1930 the door was shipped to Calvary Cemetery. The sculptor, James Novelli, then sent a letter to the Roman Bronze Works on May 22nd giving them permission to destroy the model for the Bernard F. Golden mausoleum door. [51]

Yet, the saga doesn't end here. A year later, on April 16, 1931, Bernard Golden wrote the Roman Bronze Works with a few complaints of his own: Mr. Golden stated that they were to put bronze door-knobs on both the inside and outside of the door; the key for the door was weak; also the door caught in the jambs, and you had to use considerable force to open it. Furthermore, he suggested that they look into the matter of the hinges, because someone could remove the pins and steal the door.[52] After searching their records and trying to locate the blueprints on file, the Roman Bronze Works, on December 31, 1931, responded to Mr. Golden's complaint. Having examined the approved drawing, they could not find anywhere any indication that they were told to provide bronze knobs on both the inside and outside of the door. As for the key, it was a standard knife key that was usually provided for mausoleum doors and a different type could not be installed without considerable expense. Since the door had been installed almost two years prior, the door and jambs were probably now out of line and needed to be readjusted. Finally, to install pivots, not hinges, would be entirely impractical, since they have "installed hundreds of mausoleum doors but have never heard of an instance where a door has been stolen."[53]

In yet a separate incident, a mystery seems to have surrounded a commission undertaken by James Novelli for a mausoleum door. In the early months of 1930, Mr. A.F. Krenkel, an employee and representative of the Memorials Art Company, contracted James Novelli to execute a clay model for a mausoleum door and requested that it be submitted to the Roman Bronze Works for casting in bronze. For the Krenkel commission, Novelli created an expressively moving and sensitive sculptural piece of two grief-stricken women, one consoling the other (fig. 45). In a routine manner the foundry was contacted for a cost estimate and by the third week of March the Roman Bronze Works received a letter from Mr. Krenkel confirming the commission and agreeing to a sum of $975.00, which included the frame, saddle, lock and necessary hardware.[54] In their follow-up letter dated June 9, 1930, the Roman Bronze Works, not hearing from Mr. Krenkel, wrote a letter to the Memorials Art Company, addressed to his attention, wanting to know when to expect the model at the foundry. But to their surprise and confusion they received a reply from D. Kinsley, the President of the Memorials Art Company. He stated that his firm knew nothing about the order Mr. Krenkel placed nor had he the authority whatsoever to order any material in their name. Furthermore, Mr. Krenkel was no longer an employee of the firm. The letter went on to say that "Mr. Krenkel did several things we did not like and for that reason we had to let him go and probably this is some more of his work."[55] The Memorials Art Company assured the Roman Bronze Works that they had no idea for whom or what purpose the mausoleum door was intended. The foundry officially cancelled the job on June 14, 1930. It is interesting to note that James Novelli, did eventually execute a bronze mausoleum door with a similar theme to the one that was cancelled, with, of course, some variations (fig. 46). Unfortunately, the whereabouts of this bronze door is unknown.

Novelli, would sometimes explore alternate styles for his memorials to accommodate a growing taste for the new modernism. Although still retaining the traditional classical figure, he incorporates it into a more geometric and simple design: the "Art Deco" style (fig. 47). "Art Deco," a term used to refer to a mix of styles from the 1920s and 1930s, infuses the style of an everyday world into one of elegance and sophistication. Although this style is generally associated with the field of architecture, it can easily be found across all the applied arts, including sculpture. This untitled memorial demonstrates a geometric pattern of lines echoing throughout the background stele and continuing to reverberate in the folds in the garment on the female figure. The memorial, though more streamlined in design, is no less poignant than his more elaborate, traditional mausoleum doors. The sensuous face of the seated female is bent in sorrow, expressing a melancholy charm, suggestive of the ideal features which Novelli employs in his female figures.

Works found in Catholic cemeteries outside the New York City area include: a bronze mausoleum door commissioned in 1921 for the *Bingham* family (fig. 48), a collaboration with the architect Gilbert Stanley Underwood, in the Cemetery of the Gate of Heaven, Hawthorne, New York, and a pair of bronze panels created in 1924 for the *McSwigan Memorial* (fig. 49), located in Calvary Catholic Cemetery, Pittsburgh, Pennsylvania.

Since 1817, the Trustees of St. Patrick's Cathedral have been charged with the responsibility and maintenance of both Calvary Cemetery, Queens and the Cemetery of the Gate of Heaven. Through this association, the members of the clergy of the Archdiocese of New York were for the most part familiar with Novelli's work through the many bronze memorials and mausoleum doors he had created for those cemeteries. As a sculptor and Roman Catholic, Novelli was on friendly terms with many members of the clergy, both within and outside the New York City area.[56] Through word of mouth and recommendations he received many commissions for religious statues, such as *Madonna & Child* (fig. 50), now in a private collection in South Norwalk, Connecticut and his sculpture of the *Virgin Mary* (fig. 51). On several occasions he was also commissioned to create sculptural portraits commemorating important figures within the church *Untitled* [Prelate of the Roman Catholic Church] (fig. 52), *Relief of Pope* (fig. 53),[57] and *Untitled* [Prelate of the Roman Catholic Church/Standing] (fig. 54). Novelli's seated prelate was enthroned upon a tiered pedestal to inspire respect for the sitter's position within the ranks of the clergy (fig. 55). In this work he concentrates carefully on details of the figure, the garments and the brocaded chair; his audience especially admired this naturalism and honesty of form. Novelli made these two qualities the basis for the aesthetics of his portrait sculptures.

An earlier memorial of Novelli's commissioned for a cemetery in the South is the beautiful *Thurman Memorial* (fig. 56), located in historic Oakland Cemetery, Atlanta, Georgia. It is the final resting-place of Mary Glover Thurman who died in 1916. Her desire was to be buried in a mausoleum, but if that was not possible she requested that the executor of her will, her nephew Rolfe Glover, choose something appropriate that would represent how she had lived her life. Mary and her husband Fendal enjoyed flowers and were amateur horticulturists. Her husband was a city councilman and dentist. In fact, Fendal

Thurman, is credited with naming Atlanta's famous Peachtree Street. After her husband died Mary immersed herself in her gardening and is best known for her charitable volunteer work. She would travel to area hospitals, visiting the sick and dying, bringing them flowers that she had grown in her garden. She was given the nickname "Angel." Evidently, it was for this reason that the theme of an angel was chosen to memorialize her final resting-place. The life-sized angel is depicted in the form of a majestic female sitting atop a casket decorated with a bas-relief of morning glories, these flowers meaning farewell. Both the angel and the casket are recessed into a niche. The memorial is a stop on the cemetery's walking tour and is generally described simply as a replica of Daniel Chester French's *Kinsley Memorial* in the Bronx.[58]

Other successful works of Novelli's commissioned prior to 1923, for cemeteries outside of New York, include two memorials titled *Motherhood Group* and *Rock of Ages*, both in Durham, North Carolina.[59]

37. ***Memorial Door, Hon. Peter Schmuck***, 1921, Woodlawn Cemetery, New York. Mausoleum door: Bronze painted brown with polished gold 84"x36".

38. ***Memorial to Thomas James Stewa***rt, 1923, Woodlawn Cemetery, New York. Sculpture: Bronze 6'6"x2'x2' (Base, pink granite). (Courtesy, The Architectural League of New York).

39. **Rowan Panel**, c 1920, Woodlawn Cemetery, New York. Relief panel: Bronze 36"x29".

40. **Memorial Door, Edward Siegma**n, 1920, Woodlawn Cemetery, New York. Mausoleum door: Bronze 84"x36".

41. ***Memorial Door, John Lordi, Esq.***, 1924, Calvary Cemetery, New York. Mausoleum door: Bronze 42"x84".

42. **Memorial Door, DeSalvio**, 1937, Calvary Cemetery, New York.
Mausoleum door: Bronze 41"x79".

43. *Memorial Door, Antonio Latorraca*, 1938, Calvary Cemetery, New York. Mausoleum door: Bronze 51"x103".

44. **Memorial Door, Bernard F. Golden**, 1930, Calvary Cemetery, New York. Mausoleum door: Bronze 40"x79".

45. ***Krenkel Mausoleum Door***, 1930, Mausoleum door: Clay 40"x80".
(Photo courtesy of the Roman Bronze Works Archives, Amon Carter
Museum Archives #1377).

46. **Untitled** [Two Women] Whereabouts unknown. Mausoleum door: Bronze. (Photo courtesy of the Peter A. Juley & Son Collection, Smithsonian American Art Museum #J0115523).

47. **Untitled** [Memorial Stele] Whereabouts unknown. (Photo courtesy of the Peter A. Juley & Son Collection, Smithsonian American Art Museum #J0115524).

48. ***Memorial Door, Bingham***, 1921, Cemetery of the Gate of Heaven, Hawthorne, New York. Mausoleum door: Bronze 39"x78".

49. Detail, *McSwigan Memorial*, 1924, Calvary Catholic Cemetery, Pittsburgh, Pennsylvania. Pair of Relief Panels: Bronze, 30"x21" each.

50. **Madonna & Child**, Prior to 1929, South Norwalk, Connecticut (Private Collection). (Photo courtesy of the Peter A. Juley & Son Collection, Smithsonian American Art Museum #J0115515).

51. *Untitled* [Virgin Mary] Whereabouts unknown. (Photo courtesy of the Peter A. Juley & Son Collection, Smithsonian American Art Museum #J0115527).

52. **Untitled** [Prelate of the Roman Catholic Church] Whereabouts unknown. Portrait bust: Bronze. (Photo courtesy of the Peter A. Juley & Son Collection, Smithsonian American Art Museum #J0115512).

53. Detail, **Relief of Pope**, Whereabouts unknown. Portrait bust. (Photo courtesy of the Peter A. Juley & Son Collection, Smithsonian American Art Museum #J0115520).

54. **Untitled** [Prelate of the Roman Catholic Church/Standing]
Whereabouts unknown. (Photo courtesy of the Peter A. Juley & Son
Collection, Smithsonian American Art Museum #J0115490).

55. *Untitled* [Prelate of the Roman Catholic Church/Seated] Whereabouts unknown. (Photo courtesy of the Peter A. Juley & Son Collection, Smithsonian American Art Museum #J0115511).

56. ***Thurman Memorial*** [Mary Glover Thurman], c 1916, Oakland Cemetery, Atlanta, Georgia. Sculpture: Pink Marble 6'6"x7'8"x2' (Pedestal 2'9"x7'9"x2'3"). (Photograph by Kevin Kuharic, President, Gate City Caretakers).

10

HARD TIMES AND THE WPA

A S the pendulum swings, so does the American economy, and as the *Roaring Twenties* progressed the Great Depression was waiting in the wings. American civic support for public statuary began waning throughout the 1930s. By the middle of the decade, apart from some overdue war memorials, the commemorative monument was no longer popular.[60] The shift in public taste, especially in New York, is demonstrated by the fact that funds collected for a memorial in Central Park lay dormant for years before eventually being used to create borough playgrounds. Commissions dwindled to a trickle except those that were being dispensed by the Works Progress Administration (WPA), which some artists felt were based more on politics than an appreciation for art. Reactions to the WPA vacillated from praise to criticism, depending on the observer's political viewpoint. Those opposed to the WPA regarded the project as a "frivolous boondoggle, nurturing a leftist nest of vipers."[61]

In 1930, Novelli's name was dropped from the membership rolls of the National Sculpture Society.[62] No reason was given on his membership card; present-day opinion holds that he either simply let his dues expire or was not interested in renewing his membership. During this time, the Public Works of Art Projects (PWAP) provided sporadic relief work for experienced artists, employing their talents in the conservation of public sculpture for the City of New York Parks Department. Artists were selected on the basis of their need for employment plus their professional ability. When on September 3, 1935, there was need to repair the palm leaf on the Saratoga Park *Victory* monument, a Parks Department memo stated that, "Mr. J. Novelli has been assigned to take charge of this work, being the sculptor of the monument. His suggestions are worthy of consideration. He is being transferred from the *Firemen's Memorial*, where he was an acting foreman." The memo continues to describe the work that needed to be done: plaster model to be made of palm leaf suitable for bronze casting. Bronze cleaned with detergent and to be repatinated. Granite cleaned. Repointing if necessary.[63] Records from laborer cards of the restoration team of the Parks Department indicate that "James Novelli, assistant sculptor, was discharged September 6, 1935." This was common practice when a particular task was completed. Novelli was then reassigned to work on other projects, but it is possible that he was called back when more extensive work took place on the Saratoga Park *Victory* monument between March 29, and May 5, 1937.

After the demise of the PWAP, funds were then allocated to the WPA Federal Art Project, which provided jobs for artists on the relief rolls. The WPA/FAP was highly selective and employed relatively few artists. According to personnel records, on November 30, 1935, the New York City sculpture division employed a total of 123 persons, including a supervisor, two office employees, and 120 sculptors.[64] Each state had its own director, administrative staff and artists. Artists interested in participating needed to apply to a panel of their peers. In New York, the head of the committee determined the eligibility of each artist; in the field of sculpture it was Girolamo Piccoli. Artists employed by the WPA/FAP received a basic wage range from $23.50 to $35.00 per week; supervisors were paid more. Sculptors were expected to turn in a work within a specified number of weeks or to work a number of days on a sculptural project. Generally, it was common practice for sculptors to work out of their own studios. Except for direct commissions, more often than not, the artists were free to choose their own subject matter.

Faded images on microfilm from the Smithsonian's WPA Photograph Collection provide us with a glimpse of some of the projects that Novelli worked on for the Federal Art Project.[65] A most ambitious work, which I call *Three Ages of Woman* (fig. 57), a clay model of a pediment sculpture, and another of a water fountain I call *The Water Bearer* (fig. 58), are two works created for the WPA. Novelli created two versions of the *Water Bearer*, one with the figure atop a tall column and a second sculpture where he eliminated the column. Water fountains were a recurring theme during this period (figs. 59 & 60).

Unless specifically commissioned, the majority of the sculptural works created by these unemployed artists were meant to beautify civic buildings and especially public parks. Unfortunately, there is no mention about the whereabouts of these sculptures or even if they were ever completed; such as in the case of the *Sphinx* (fig. 61). The clearest documentation of the existence of these sculptural commissions comes from the photographs taken by the commercial photographer Paul Juley, in the sculptor's studio. The Peter A. Juley & Son collection at the Smithsonian American Art Museum is a photographic archive that documents the work of over 10,000 American artists. Specializing in American Art, his business was in operation from 1896 to 1975.[66] Although of great historical significance, the Juley collection of photographs is solely concerned with the images; unfortunately, they do not contain detailed information about the works or their whereabouts.

Another complication arises from the fact that many of Novelli's works created for the WPA have either been destroyed or displaced over the years, as was the case with a pair of relief tablets in the Fordham Hospital, Bronx, New York, which was torn down in July 1977. Unfortunately, although the

Sculpture Project, associated with the WPA, placed many of the sculptures in public places, the majority of the non-allocated works were stored by the WPA in storage rooms, only to be lost over the years or eventually sold off by the pound. It is also a fact that in 1943, the final days of the New York WPA/FAP, project records that were scheduled to be shipped to Washington D.C., disappeared without a trace.[67]

On December 15, 1936, at the age of 51, James Novelli filed for a Social Security account number and on his application he wrote "Unemployed, WPA" as his employer. Very little is mentioned about Novelli after this date. He maintained his studio on West Twenty-third Street throughout the lean years, but was forced to give it up in 1939. Hard times were nothing new for most Americans, but what made this period unique was the large scale of suffering and the length of time it lasted: people were beginning to feel that the Depression would never go away. In the first two years following the Stock Market crash the suicide rate rose over thirty percent.

Apparently despondent over the lack of new commissions, and alarmed about the war conditions in Europe, Novelli took his own life at the age of fifty-four on the afternoon of May 31, 1940. His wife Lillian came home from work to find that James, alone in their apartment, had hanged himself with a clothesline thrown over the transom of a bathroom door.[68] She quickly cut him down and lowered his body to the bathroom floor. There were no signs of life but she summoned an ambulance from Flushing Hospital. When it arrived, the intern could only pronounce the sculptor dead. On June 3rd James Novelli was laid to rest, under a simple headstone, in Calvary Cemetery, Queens, the same cemetery that accommodates many of his most elaborate and exquisite sculptural works.

For over sixty years, the artist and his works remained obscure. It took the criminal deeds of two blundering thieves, stealing the sculpture of *Victory*, to bring his name to light once more. It is ironic that this was the same sculpture that originally brought him recognition and fame from the general public back in 1921.

57. **Untitled** [Three Ages of Woman] Whereabouts unknown. Pediment Sculpture: Clay Model. (Photo courtesy of the Peter A. Juley & Son Collection, Smithsonian American Art Museum #J0115516).

58. *Untitled* [Water Bearer] Whereabouts unknown. Sculpture. (Photo courtesy of the Peter A. Juley & Son Collection, Smithsonian American Art Museum #J0115502).

59. *Untitled* [Cherubs with Fish] Whereabouts unknown. Sculpture: Plaster cast. (Photo courtesy of the Peter A. Juley & Son Collection, Smithsonian American Art Museum #J0115513).

60. **Untitled** [Cherubs with Fish] Whereabouts unknown. Sculpture:
Clay model. (Photo courtesy of the Peter A. Juley & Son Collection,
Smithsonian American Art Museum #J0115507).

61. **Untitled** [Sphinx] Whereabouts unknown. Sculpture: Clay model. (Photo courtesy of the Peter A. Juley & Son Collection, Smithsonian American Art Museum #J0115514).

62. **Crucifix**, Prior to 1923, Holy Name Cemetery, Jersey City, New Jersey. Sculpture: Bronze 5'x4' (Base/Cross: Granite 9').

11

A BROTHER REMEMBERED

FOR years his family, his brothers and sisters, agonized over his suicide. They would always remember him as the thoughtful, loving son who every weekend would travel from his home in Jackson Heights, Queens, to visit his mother on Bathgate Avenue in the Bronx. Generous all his life, he would always arrive with presents in hand. His family never called him by the name of James, he was always known as John. He was the soft-spoken, "Uncle John" who would spend hours teaching his young niece Frances how to draw. She would remember him as an intelligent, mild mannered, handsome man with auburn hair and warm brown eyes, always impeccably dressed in his favorite shade of brown. James had a sweet sounding voice and the family would love to listen to him speak for he spoke so eloquently and fluently in both Italian and English.[69] He always seemed happy and confident, never giving a hint as to his inner anxiety or mental turmoil, never betraying the persona he wished to present. His youngest sister Mamie never got over his death, blaming his wife Lillian and son Jimmy for their extravagant demands. Unfortunately, the union between Lillian and James had not been a happy marriage. It was said of Lillian that she liked, wanted and demanded the finer things in life.[70] During the prosperous years her husband would try to make her happy by bringing her expensive presents, surprising her on one occasion with a matching necklace and bracelet made up of gold coins.[71] Mamie once wrote of her brother, "My beloved brother John, who was God-gifted at this profession, but unlucky in his life with his family."[72]

James' mother Lucia, lived in the home of her youngest daughter at the time of the suicide but was never told of her son's death. The family feared that at the age of 80, she was too fragile, and tried to shield her from such agony; instead they told her that he had to return to Italy on business. Lucia always questioned that story and never fully believed that her son would leave without saying goodbye. On a few occasions after James' death, Lillian would bring their son Jimmy, then age 16, to visit his grandmother. Each time Mamie would leave the room wanting nothing to do with her sister-in-law; she found the anguish unbearable and didn't want her mother to see her this way.

In due course, Lillian gave up the apartment on 95th Street in Jackson Heights, along with the memories which resided within, and moved away to be closer to her own family in Corona, Queens. A neighbor from Corona, who knew Lillian and Jimmy after they had moved to 102nd Street, remembers that she continued to work for the Chiclets Chewing Gum Company. She had worked at Chiclets during the Depression and helped support the family when James was alive; she was making a good salary and held a position of responsibility, as secretary to an executive of the company. After her husband's untimely death she managed to support both Jimmy and herself in a comfortable manner. She was described as a very attractive woman, with a good sense of humor and one who enjoyed having a good time. The neighbor recalled that she would "dress to the nines," always leaving for work impeccably attired.[73] The children of the neighborhood would enjoy seeing her and wait for her to come home because she always had a supply of little packets of Chiclets Chewing Gum for them.

There was no consoling Mamie for the death of her brother. She would always blame Lillian for her reckless spending, which Mamie felt contributed strongly to her brother's suicide. It was just a matter of time before the two families, Mamie's and Lillian's, finally split for good. Eventually, over the years, Mamie and her family would lose track of the whereabouts of Lillian and Jimmy. It was through Social Security records that it was learned, only recently, about the death of James (Jimmy) Novelli in February 1999.

Mamie would spend much of her life mourning her favorite brother; trying to keep his memory alive through newspaper clippings and photographs, anything that she could find. She was hurting emotionally and could never understand why no one ever took an interest to write about her brother. How could someone, with so much talent, be forgotten so quickly? After Lucia's death, Mamie and her family moved to New Jersey. It was there, many years later, that Mamie's husband Frank died and was buried in Holy Name Cemetery in Jersey City. Each week Mamie would travel to the cemetery to visit and tend to the grave of her husband, passing on her way a prominent bronze crucifix. In 1986 Mamie passed away and was buried next to her husband. It's both sad and ironic that Mamie never knew in her lifetime that the nine-foot bronze *Crucifix,* marking the graves of the Sisters of St. Joseph (fig. 62), in Holy Name Cemetery, had been sculpted by her beloved brother James.

12

IN RETROSPECT

I T was not just the economic aspect of the Great Depression
that tolled the "death of public monuments." The ascen-
dancy of the modernist sculptors, their unwillingness to produce monuments commemorating World War I, and modern
public opinion's rejection of the traditional glorification of
events and individuals, all contributed heavily toward the di-
minishing demand for public monuments. The activities of the
modernists expanded and by the twenties they had gained
much more widespread support. New institutions such as the
Whitney Museum of Art and the Museum of Modern Art, promoted innovative modernist styles and posed a serious chal-
lenge to the older society like the National Sculpture Society.[74]
The social philosopher Lewis Mumford, in 1938, described it
more simply: "If it is a monument, it is not modern, and if it is
modern, it cannot be a monument."[75]

As it happened, James Novelli was caught in a dilemma
created by society and the political era in which he lived. The
production of civic projects was initiated and supported by a
small number of urban elite who shared the same concerns and
ideals as those of the sculptors. If a sculptor was ambitious and
determined to be successful he had to compete for commissions, which meant his priorities were directed toward patron
satisfaction. Generally, large public allegorical monuments
were commissioned, not by the general public, but mostly by a
municipal department of the city. Established standards defined

what constituted good public sculpture; unity of representation and academic symbolism prevailed among sculptures, only allowing for minor deviations stemming from the personal touch of the artist. These stylistic conventions, endorsed by the National Sculpture Society, played a big part in public sculptures. The problem was that academic symbolism, its meaning and the allegorical ideal it was meant to convey was often lost on the masses. These allegorical symbols were not always well received by the average audience, causing the relationship between the public and the sculptor to become strained. The privileged position of the sculptor as a professional began to be questioned and ultimately began to wane.

Architects indisputably played a major role in promoting public monuments and at one time the architectural firms depended heavily upon sculptural design created by sculptors who were trained in the European schools of the fine arts. Preferences in the architectural field, after the 1920s, began to change as many younger architects started to embark upon projects that were sculpturally less ambitious, compared to those of an earlier period. At the same time, there was a growing trend whereby ornamental detail mainly utilized in commercial and residential buildings was being produced by American trained ornamental modelers. The young architects felt that these fully trained modelers and carvers could perform the work just as well as the professional sculptors. Architects would no longer need to form collaborations with sculptors; this inevitably placed the architect, and not the sculptor, in control of the sculptural needs best suited for their designs. It also meant there was no longer a need to deal with the principles of the National Sculpture Society, with its old foundations of cultural authority, nor to submit to the demands of the individual sculptor. Released from these artistic restraints, architects found new opportunities to demonstrate their own independent expression and were now free to take a more active role in the decision making of the sculptural design.[76]

In retrospect, the *Gilded Age* and the 1920s together formed an extensive, exuberant economic period that in reality could not be sustained indefinitely. The organizational structure that supported public monuments had diminished by the end of the 1920s. Owing to the growing instability of the economy, elite groups, which at one time promoted large-scale civic sculptures, now withdrew their support. Coupled to this was the decrease in public enthusiasm for allegorical ideals, which had pervaded throughout the early decades of the twentieth century and now culminated in a rapidly growing trend of rejection. James Novelli was but one participant in this inflated interval of sculptural history; unfortunately, he was not alone. There were many, many more sculptors active during that era who must have experienced the same heights and depths as Novelli, but their names will remain anonymous and their stories will remain untold until scholarly studies bring them to light.

NOTES & SOURCES

[1] *SIRIS*: *Smithsonian Institution Research Information System*, Home Page, <http://www.siris.si.edu> (29 January 2002), "Art Inventories," Browse Artists, Novelli, James, Control No IAS 76003593 (hereinafter cited, Art inventories / Control number).

[2] Shaila Dewan, "2 Are Charged After Police Find Stolen Statue in 300 Pieces," *New York Times*, 24 April 2000, B5:2.

[3] Robert Ingrassia, "Commish Vows Statue Solution," *Daily News* (New York), 25 April 2000, 8.

[4] Glen B. Opitz, ed., "Novelli, James," *Dictionary of American Sculptors: 18th Century to the Present* (Poughkeepsie: Apollo, 1984), 296.

[5] Opitz, "Novelli," *Dictionary of American Sculptors*, 296.

[6] Felix Novelli, telephone conversation with author, 23 January 2001. Felix is a nephew of the sculptor James Novelli and the son of Charles Novelli. He was able to provide firsthand recollections about the sculptor, his wife Lillian and their son Jimmy.

[7] Felix Novelli, telephone conversation.

[8] Michael and Felix Melfa, interviewed by author, tape recorded, 07 January 2001. Michael and Felix are the nephews of the sculptor James Novelli and the sons of Mamie Melfa, the sculptor's youngest sister. Felix Melfa, although younger than Jimmy Novelli, recounted family gatherings and remembered firsthand information about his famous uncle. Michael Melfa was born the year James Novelli died. Michael was able to provide information regarding conversations he overheard as a child growing up and memories that were handed down from his mother Mamie. Michael has a strong interest in researching the works of his uncle and has spent many

hours putting together an album of newspaper clippings collected by his mother and photos of the sculptor's works.

[9] Opitz, "Novelli," *Dictionary of American Sculpture*, 296.

[10] *SIRIS: Smithsonian Institution Research Information System*, "Art Inventories," General Keyword: "Chief Menominee", Control No. IAS IN001074.

[11] James W. Loewen, *Lies Across AMERICA: What Our Historic Sites Get Wrong* (New York: The New Press, 1999), 146.

[12] Jane Turner, ed., "Giulio Monteverde." vol. 22, *The Dictionary of Art* (New York: Grove's Dictionaries, 1996), 22.

[13] Art Inventories / Control No: IAS NJ000200.

[14] "Roses Fall on Monument," *New York Times*, 05 July 1922, 21:7. (For further information on this monument, go to: *Jersey City Monuments,* <http://www.rootsweb.com/~njhudson/JC/monuments.htm>)

[15] "Unveil Bedford Memorial," *New York Times*, 12 September 1921, 13:5.

[16] Quoted in Tom Armstrong, et al, *200 Years of American Sculpture* (New York: David R. Godine, Publisher, 1976), 114-115.

[17] Michele H. Bogart, *Public Sculpture and the Civic Ideal in New York City, 1890-1930* (Chicago: The University of Chicago Press, 1989), 50-51.

[18] National Sculpture Society, *Exhibition of American Sculpture Guide: April 14th–August 1st,* rev. ed, 03 May 1923 (New York: National Sculpture Society), Novelli's three entries included a Mausoleum door, # 618; Sir Walter Raleigh (sketch), # 635, War Memorial (sketch), # 643.

[19] National Sculpture Society, *Contemporary American Sculpture: the California Palace of the Legion of Honor, Lincoln Park, San Francisco, April-October, MCMXXIX* (New York: Press of the Kalkhoff Company, 1929), 244.

[20] Bogart, *Public Sculpture*, 82-85.

[21] Sarah Carr-Gromm, *Dictionary of Symbols in Western Art* (New York: Facts on File, 1995), 31, 136, 166.

[22] The Art Commission is the New York City agency that is responsible for the review and approval of works of art on City-owned property. (For further information on this agency go to: *Art Commission of the City of New York*, Home Page, 01 January 2002, <http://nyc.gov/html/artcom/home.html>, Intro to Commission).

[23] James Novelli, Work Of Art Form, submission no. 3279, sent to the Art Commission of the City of New York, dated 15 January 1926. James Novelli Files, Art Commission of the City of New York Archives (hereinafter cited, Novelli /submission # / dated / Art Commission).

[24] Novelli / submission no. 2688 / dated 13 March 1922 /Art Commission.

[25] Novelli / submission no. 3493 / dated 8 July 1927 / Art Commission.

[26] Novelli / submission no. 3518 / dated 13 September 1927 / Art Commission.

[27] Art Inventories / Control No. IAS IN000781.

[28] *Veterans Memorial Park*, "Site of Lockport's Historic Soldier's Monument," <http://www.lockport-ny.com/Tourism/parks8.htm> (28 February 2001).

[29] Michael Melfa, interview. Mr. Melfa, related to me that his father Frank Melfa, often worked part-time as a studio assistant for his brother-in-law James Novelli, and on several occasions was witness to Novelli taking a hammer to his work and destroying it totally because he was not fully satisfied with the results.

[30] Peter Hastings Falk, ed., vol. 3, *The Annual Exhibition record of the Pennsylvania Academy of the Fine Arts* (Madison, CT: Sound View Press, 1988-1989), 348. According to this index the bust of *Peter Anderson* was shown from 25 January to 15 March 1931at the 126th Annual Exhibition of the Pennsylvania Academy of the Fine Arts, along with his sculpture *Torso*.

[31] James Novelli, in a letter to the Hon. Joseph S. Frelinghuysen (President of the Harding Memorial Association), dated 19 July 1924. Harding Memorial Files, Ohio Historical Society. Novelli is requesting that consideration be given to him in reference to a bust that he had sculpted of the late President for the Harding Memorial. Novelli also states the disposition of a copy of the Harding bust to the *Marion Star* newsroom. [So far, the Historical

Society has been unable to determine where the bust went from there. The whereabouts of the bust remains a mystery].

[32] The relief bust of Francis P. DeLuna, was shown in the "Exhibition of Sculpture under the auspices of the National Sculpture Society." Whitney Museum, April 03–May 02, 1940.

[33] NSS, *Contemporary American Sculpture*, 245. The majority of these sculptures are in private collections, their whereabouts unknown. As for the relief bust of James Cardinal Gibbons, although the publication states that the relief sculpture is located at the Catholic University, Washington D.C., the assistant archivist of the Catholic University, Eric Fair, informed me that they have no knowledge of the sculpture or its whereabouts.

[34] "Honor John R. Rathom," *New York Times*, 05 July 1929, 21:2

[35] General Bronze Corporation, Sales Dept., in a letter to Mr. Edward Riley, Secretary, Newark Lodge #21, 11 January 1930. Roman Bronze Works Archives Job #1260, Amon Carter Museum Archives, Ft. Worth, Texas. (hereinafter cited, RBW Archives Job # / Amon Carter Museum).

[36] A.W.Roth, General Bronze Corporation, in an inter-office memo to the Sales Department, dated 01 February 1930. RBW Archives Job #1260 / Amon Carter Museum.

[37] E.J. Buckley, Roman Bronze Works Inc., subsidiary of the General Bronze Corporation, in a letter to Edward Riley, Sec. Newark Lodge #21, 29 May 1930. RBW Archives Job #1260 / Amon Carter Museum.

[38] Shirley Katzter, telephone conversation with author, 25 September 2000. George and Shirley Katzter, were the directors of the Coleridge School Byron Campus. Not too long ago the property on Shore Boulevard was sold and a synagogue was erected on the site where once the stately mansion stood.

[39] Letter of Miss Ethel Henneford, Lincoln National Life Insurance Company, Ft. Wayne, Indiana, dated 10 July 1930. Novelli, Artist Files, New York Public Library, Art Division Microfiche Collection. It appears this letter could have been in response to a request by an unknown individual or institution trying to locate the whereabouts of the sculpture. Miss Henneford's letter states, "We have searched the various sources at our disposal and have been unable to locate the statue of Lincoln. The National Sculpture Society reports the same inability."

[40] *Architectural League of New York*, "The League," <http://www.archleague.org/league.html#> (31 May 2000), History.

[41] "Annual Exhibits in the Fine Arts," *New York Times*, 28 January 1923, IX 1:8.

[42] "Architects Award Medals at Exhibit," *New York Times*, 27 January 1923, 16:3.

[43] Edward F. Bergman, *Woodlawn Remembers: Cemetery of American History* (Utica, NY: North Country Books, Inc., 1988), 10.

[44] NSS, *Contemporary American Sculpture*, 245. Listed within Novelli's works is also a memorial titled, *LaMattina-Guerriero*, (bronze & granite), Calvary Cemetery, New York. However, as of this writing the memorial is still unlocated.

[45] Amicus Most, Jr., Roman Bronze Works Inc., in a letter to James Novelli, Sc., dated 12 March 1929, confirming their verbal estimate. RBW Archives Job #629 / Amon Carter Museum.

[46] D. Kinsley, General Manager, Memorials Art Company, Inc. in a letter to the Roman Bronze Works, dated 22 April 1929. RBW Archives Job #629 / Amon Carter Museum.

[47] Amicus Most Jr., in a letter to James Novelli, dated 14 June 1929 (a copy of the letter was sent to Mr. Bernard F. Golden, 51 Maiden Lane, NYC). RBW Archives Job #629 / Amon Carter Museum.

[48] Amicus Most, Jr., in a letter to Bernard F. Golden, dated 20 May 1929. RBW Archives Job #629 / Amon Carter Museum.

[49] Amicus Most, Jr., in a letter to Bernard F. Golden, dated 07 August 1929. RBW Archives Job #629 / Amon Carter Museum.

[50] W.J. Freeman, Accounting Dept., Roman Bronze Works, Inc., in an inter-office correspondence to R.R. Bertelli, President, dated 10 March 1930. Freeman explains that from past experience he was under the impression that this will be a prolonged account, unless they hold up shipment of the door until they received the final payment of $450.00, since Mr. Golden was very anxious to have the door shipped. RBW Archives Job #629 / Amon Carter Museum.

[51] James Novelli, in a letter to E.J. Buckley, Roman Bronze Works, Inc., dated 22 May 1930. RBW Archives Job #629 / Amon Carter Museum.

[52] Bernard F. Golden, in a letter to Roman Bronze Works, Inc., dated 16 April 1931. RBW Archives Job #629 / Amon Carter Museum.

[53] R.D. Denise, manager, Roman Bronze Works, Inc., in a letter to Bernard F. Golden, dated 31 December 1931, in response to Mr. Golden's letter of complaint. RBW Archives Job #629 / Amon Carter Museum.

[54] A.F. Krenkel, Memorials Art Company, Inc., in a letter to the Roman Bronze Works, Inc., dated 24 March 1930. RBW Archives Job #1377 / Amon Carter Museum.

[55] D. Kinsley, President of the Memorials Art Company, Inc., in a letter to F.L. Huber, Roman Bronze Works, Inc., dated 14 June 1930. RBW Archives Job #1377 / Amon Carter Museum.

[56] Michael Melfa, interview. Mr. Melfa suggested that James Novelli was on very friendly terms with many members of the clergy at St. Patrick's and would have been recommended for commissions through them.

[57] This author believes that this photo may have been mistakenly titled *Relief of Pope*, by the Peter A. Juley Collection. After performing extensive research on James Cardinal Gibbons, this author has found a strong resemblance in facial features between the profile of Cardinal Gibbons and the sculpture *Relief of Pope*. It is possible that this sculpture is the relief bust of James Cardinal Gibbons that was said to have been located at the Catholic University in Washington, D.C.

[58] Kevin Kuharic, President, Gate City Caretakers, in an e-mail to the author, dated 9 March 2002. Kevin Kuharic, over the years, has done extensive research on Historic Oakland Cemetery. He performed the research on the *Mary Glover Thurman Memorial* several years ago, as a volunteer for the Historic Oakland Foundation. The primary sources used in his research were the will of Mary Glover Thurman and the work "Atlanta and Environs," by Franklin M. Garrett. Presently, Kevin Kuharic, along with co-researcher/writer Paul T. Boat, Landscape Designer, are working on a book about Oakland Cemetery tentatively titled, "Planting Paradise."

[59] NSS, *Contemporary American Sculpture*, 245. The exact locations of these sculptures, within the city of Durham, as of yet have not been found nor are there any photos available of the works.

[60] Penelope Curtis, *Sculpture 1900-1945: after Rodin* (Oxford: Oxford University Press, 1999), 55.

[61] Greta Berman, "New York WPA Artists, Then and Now," In *New York City WPA Art*, (New York: NYC WPA Artists Inc., 1977), xvii.

[62] National Sculpture Society, James Novelli membership information, Rolodex.

[63] Karl H. Gruppe, New York City Department of Parks, in a repair memo to J.F. Walsh, 03 September 1935. James Novelli Files, New York City Department of Parks Archives.

[64] Eleanor Carr, "New York Sculpture during the Federal Art Project," *The Art Journal* XXXI:4 (summer 1972): 397.

[65] *Smithsonian Archives of American Art*, "WPA Photographic Collection," <www.archivesofamericanart.si.edu/findaids/fedartpr/fedartpr.htm> (16 March, 2002) Microfilm Reel 1170.

[66] *SIRIS: Smithsonian Institution Research Information System*, "Juley Photographic Archive," <http://www.siris.si.edu/siris-juley.htm> (14 May 2001).

[67] Norma Barr, "Statement," In *New York City WPA Art*, xiv.

[68] "Novelli, Sculptor, Ends Life in Home," *New York Times*, 01 June 1940, 32:6.

[69] Frances Melfa, telephone conversation with author, 15 January 2001. Frances is the niece of the sculptor James Novelli and the daughter of Mamie Melfa. She has related firsthand information about her Uncle John, who would spend hours teaching her how to draw.

[70] Michael Melfa, interview.

[71] Felix Novelli, telephone conversation.

[72] Mamie Melfa, wrote those words in her own hand across the bottom of newspaper clippings of her brother's works.

[73] Louis Anastasi, telephone conversation with author, 24 April 2001. Mr. Anastasi was a neighbor and friend of Jimmy Novelli when they both lived in Corona, Queens. He was also stationed with Jimmy at the Naval Base in Norfolk, Virginia, before being sent overseas during World War II.

[74] Bogart, *Public Sculpture*, 297.

[75] Lewis Mumford, *The Culture of Cities* (New York: Harcourt, Brace & Co., 1938), 438.

[76] Bogart, *Public Sculpture*, 293-297.

51799062R00074

Made in the USA
Charleston, SC
30 January 2016